Trust Your Timing

This book is dedicated to all the men who ever broke my heart. Thank you for inspiring me to look within.

Trust Your Timing

How to Use Astrology to Navigate Your Love Life

Alice Bell

Andrews McMeel
PUBLISHING®

Contents

Introduction

"When am I going to meet someone?" and "What signs am I compatible with?" are two of the most commonly asked questions I receive as a professional astrologer. In today's world, where there is currently so much uncertainty, a lot of us are looking for something that gives deeper meaning to our lives. We are trying to understand why we are the way we are, as well as what life path, jobs, or relationships might be the best fit for us, and we're hoping we can find answers to these questions by looking to astrology. In particular, the majority of people I speak to turn to astrology to navigate their love life woes and better understand their relationship dynamics.

Dating, and relationships specifically, is a point of obsession for most of us. There is a lot of pressure to be on dating apps every day or talking to multiple people at once. Dating is often described as a numbers game, and that you have to constantly be putting effort into it in order to be successful. I disagree with this mindset, though. When I tried to meet guys this way in my early to mid-twenties in New York City, I got easily burned out and discouraged. It would sometimes feel impossible to connect with people, and I would often blame myself for not saying the right things or texting back too quickly. There's also the unspoken timeline of needing to be engaged or married by a certain age, and the presumption that, if you haven't had a relationship in several years—or ever, for that matter—something must be wrong with you. It wasn't until I taught myself astrology that I was able to understand it wasn't me doing anything wrong after all; casual dating just wasn't for me, and it simply was not my time to be in a relationship.

Though astrology has been on the rise in recent years, there remains the common misconception that it's not much more than your weekly horoscope or a funny meme about your star sign. However, knowing your star sign (which is, more accurately, your sun sign) and the clichéd traits that go along with it is only the tip of the iceberg. In fact, astrology is an ancient practice, with its origins dating back to the third millennium BC in Mesopotamia. During that time period, astrologers would closely track what was happening in the sky and correlate it to events happening back on Earth. Going beyond just your "sign," you have what is called a birth chart, based on the exact time, date, and city in which you were born. It's a snapshot of where the planets were positioned in the sky at the moment you took your first breath of life.

This astrological blueprint, once you learn how to decode it, shows what your natural skill sets are and what interests you may want to lean into to feel happier, versus what areas of life might be more challenging. It can explain difficult sides to yourself, such as why you may have a strained relationship with your family or how you may battle with controlling behaviors in your relationships, while also revealing easier aspects like having a natural skill for teaching or a love of immersing yourself in foreign cultures. Understanding your unique birth chart is a powerful tool in gaining greater self-awareness. For me personally, it has been more effective than therapy.

Out of the many areas of astrology there are to discuss, I've chosen to write about love and relationships for this book. As a professional astrologer, I look at the charts of hundreds of people a year, and all anyone wants to hear about is their love life. I, myself, am equally as interested in finding out these answers. Wanting to understand my own relationships and dating patterns is what initially drew me to astrology and introduced me to the intricacies of my birth chart. I know that I am not the only person who has turned to astrology to get a little insight into what type of person my potential match might be. Too often there is the belief that if your "sign" doesn't work with someone else's, then the relationship is doomed. However, the sun sign is only *one* component of your entire birth chart, and it has little to do with intimacy and sexuality. It is only by looking at your entire birth chart that you can truly understand the full complexity of you as a person.

The best way to describe my dating behavior throughout my late teens and twenties is obsessive. I had never experienced a serious, adult relationship, but that was the one thing I wanted the most. Instead, I kept tabs on the people I liked from afar, building up a fantasy in my head that we would one day end up together, or I would try to create immediate intimacy with people, each fling ending just as fast as it started. I was always the dumpee, never the dumper, and if I sensed that the other person was trying to pull away, I would try even harder to make them stay. Being with anyone was better than being alone, no matter how many red flags there may have been. It felt like everyone else my age was able to go on several dates a week or sleep with people casually like it was no big deal, but for me, doing this was always so emotionally painful afterward. I didn't understand why I cared so much, and why I started fantasizing about every guy I went on even one date with as my future husband.

In January of 2018, I happened upon astrology because of yet another failed romantic encounter. During that winter, I was still engaging in the same dating patterns I had been repeating my entire life without ever considering that I could change this side of myself. The most recent drama was that someone I had been messaging with a year prior had finally come back and texted me late one night asking to see me again. Of course, I dropped everything I was doing to rush over to his apartment. It ended exactly as it had before, and when I left his place the next day, I never heard a word from him again. In the weeks that followed, I held out hope that he would text me. I knew little to nothing about astrology then, but when work was slow, I searched our astrological compatibility, and I read my daily horoscope religiously, looking for clues that he might reach out again. Wanting to ignore all the red flags once again, I was hoping that astrology would validate my decision to wait around for someone who was clearly not interested. Though I wasn't able to find any concrete answers to this particular dating dilemma, my Google searches did lead me down a rabbit hole of astrological information and, somehow, I ended up entering in my exact time, date, and city of birth into an astrology website to generate my personal birth chart.

Before this moment, all I knew was that my sun sign was Aquarius. Traits associated with Aquarius are being emotionally aloof and cold, a bit rebellious, and very independent, with a need for their own space. While parts of Aquarius resonated, it didn't fully explain my specific dating behavior, especially the clinginess, the low self-esteem, and the need to give and give to the wrong types of people. Upon researching further into my birth chart, I realized that I had both my moon and Venus in Pisces in the eighth house. These placements explained why, when I liked someone, I would get fixated on them, and why I harbored secret crushes for years. In addition, I learned that I had Saturn in the seventh house, which meant that a committed relationship was more likely to come in my late twenties or early thirties, and that I needed a relationship where my partner took commitment just as seriously as I did. My birth chart spelled out what I had failed to face within myself for my whole life. I was someone who needed intensity and could not keep things casual, no matter how hard I tried. I felt relieved, knowing that there was nothing wrong with me, and that I had these traits for a reason.

Somehow, a guy not texting me back spurred an entire career change. Already feeling unfulfilled in my job as a fashion assistant at *Vogue*, I started to spend all my downtime at work and any other free moments teaching myself astrology. Astrology helped calm me down, especially in regard to my love life, and I wanted everyone around me to realize it could do the same for them, too. Now, five years into my practice as an astrologer, I still love the feeling that comes when I identify something in a client's chart that suggests why they may be having difficulties, and they smile and say, "Yes, that's spot on."

Astrology is also useful when it comes to recognizing there is a timing for everything. From the age of 22 until 28, I was completely single. Whereas in college I had always had someone around, during this stretch of my twenties I had no situationships, and no one got past five dates. I used to spend a lot of energy swiping on dating apps, getting more and more frustrated when nothing worked out. It felt like I had to be constantly searching for someone and putting myself out there for a relationship to happen. I often compared myself to people who had met their future husband in college or had magically been introduced to someone through a friend, and I didn't understand why that never happened to me. As I learned more about astrology and its predictive powers, I was able to see what year a relationship was most likely to occur.

In astrology, not only do you have a birth chart, which gives clues into your personality, but based on where the planets are currently positioned in the sky, different parts of your life and your identity will become more emphasized over time. When relationship-focused houses and planets in your chart are activated (meaning the current movement of the planets are aligned with parts of your chart for a set amount of time), it is likely that you will enter into a relationship. It works the other way, too. If there is nothing currently going in the relationship sectors of your chart, then even if you do decide to keep putting all of your energy into dating, it is unlikely that anything will stick. There are simply certain years where being in a relationship is the focus, while there are other years where it isn't. Knowing the timing of my own chart took the pressure off having to always be looking for someone, and I could shift my focus elsewhere, like becoming a better astrologer or strengthening my friendships or family relationships. I deleted the dating apps and spent the next three years alone, as a kind of test to see if something would come along. I knew that 2021 would be my year to meet someone, but despite the happy relationship updates I received from my clients, I still wasn't entirely convinced that it would happen for me.

In late January 2021, still in the midst of a Covid lockdown when I was barely leaving my apartment, I had an Instagram follower message me. "I know this sounds strange, but I weirdly think you'd like my friend (if you're single). If you're interested let me know!" I had never exchanged messages with her, but I said yes, because I knew from astrology that this was the year I needed to be open to meeting new people. She had also sent me his entire birth chart (Taurus sun, Scorpio moon, and Sagittarius rising), and, when I saw he had a Scorpio moon, I knew he would have the same emotional intensity as me, and that we would have a lot to talk about. Had I simply googled "Are Taurus and Aquarius compatible?" it would have said no. I had to take his entire chart into consideration to see if we might connect. While I usually don't recommend looking at your date's chart before meeting them because it can lead to obsessing over whether you're compatible with someone's signs and placements, in this case I broke my own rules—and it worked! That first date was the start of our relationship, and we've been together ever since.

I tell this story not to show that all my problems were solved by meeting someone, but to demonstrate that astrological timing and compatibility are real, and that there's more to it than what is commonly believed. When I trusted my timing, I no longer spent my days fixating on when I might get a boyfriend. Instead, I accepted that serious romance was probably not in the cards for me until 2021, and I was able to excel in other areas of my life. Throughout this book, I'll show you how you can do the same.

How to Read This Book

IN THE FIRST part of this book, we will go over what a birth chart is, going through how you can pull it up and begin reading your chart. I will also briefly cover what the zodiac signs mean, as well as the signification of each planet and house of the chart. Once we have a firm grasp on beginner-level astrology, we will then begin decoding birth charts through the lens of relationships. If you're new to astrology, there will be lots to learn, but we will go slowly and figure it out step by step together. If you're already familiar with your chart and want to take your knowledge to the next level, this introduction will still be helpful to recap the basics and understand my particular style of astrology before we head into Part Two.

Oftentimes, there is a tendency to get caught up in what everyone else is doing dating-wise, without considering what you really want. So, in the second part of this book, I want you to forget about looking to see if you're compatible with another person, and work on becoming more aware of your own dating patterns. We will be focusing on the parts of your chart that specifically pertain to relationships and intimacy, so you will better understand what you want and need out of a relationship, using your birth chart as a map to gain greater self-awareness. Then, at the end of this section, we'll also look at how to navigate placements in your birth chart that can make relationships more challenging. I want to stress here that nothing in astrology means you are doomed in love, but that there may just be more challenges for you to overcome than there are for others. There's no need to panic, because with every challenging chart placement, there is always the potential to master that part of your life and make it work to your advantage.

In the third part, I will show you how to determine compatibility and will demonstrate a couple of different ways you can compare your chart to someone else's. Rather than listing what signs work for you and what signs don't, I will dive into how a synastry chart (the comparison of two birth charts by overlaying one on top of the other) shows where, as a couple, you may face challenges, as well as where the relationship's strengths may lie. I will be debunking the myth that all of a couple's signs have to match up perfectly in order for a relationship to work by giving examples of common configurations I see in the charts of long-term couples. What we cover in this part can also be applied when comparing your chart to a friend's or family member's, so this will help you understand all relationships in your life, not just the romantic ones. Astrology should be seen as a helpful tool to better relate to people, rather than something that determines the fate of a relationship.

And finally, in the last part, we will get a glimpse into what your next romantic move might be, whether that's meeting someone, moving in with your partner, getting married, or even undergoing a stressful break-up. There is a lot of pressure from society to meet major relationship milestones by a certain age, when in reality that timing is completely out of our control. Relationships come along when they are meant to, and when this might happen is what astrology is able to show. In this section, I will be introducing predictive astrology, specifically how the current movement of the planets in relation to your birth chart can show when you may date more frequently or develop greater commitment with your partner. On the other hand, there are also periods where relationships go through stress, causing you to feel distant from your partner, or times when you might be met with a handful of painful dating experiences. I will point out how to identify these more difficult periods and determine how long they might last. While astrology can't show the exact person you may meet, or if a relationship will result specifically in marriage or a break-up, it is calming to know that there are years when big love life developments will happen and years when they won't. Everything really is all up to divine timing.

I want you to walk away from this book with an understanding that astrology is a helpful tool in improving your relationships and developing greater self-awareness when dating, rather than dismissing certain signs based on common clichés. By the end of this book, you will be able to identify your specific relationship patterns, understand underlying dynamics between you and the people in your life, and have a better idea of the natural cycles that dating and relationships go through. No matter what stage of life you're in, there is something to be learned from interpreting your astrological chart and uncovering different sides to yourself. Think of reading this book as another simple act of self-care. If you're ready, let's get started on this journey together.

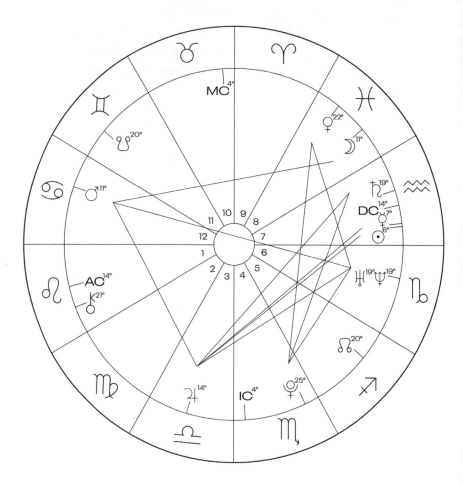

My birth chart.

PART ONE

Where It All Begins: Your Birth Chart

Now that we've discussed that there is more to astrology beyond just your "star sign," let's break down the various components of your birth chart. To recap, everyone has what is called a birth chart, which is essentially a snapshot of the sky at the moment you took your first breath of life.

Looking at your birth chart may feel overwhelming at first, with all of the various glyphs and lines, so I will be walking you through how to interpret each element, step by step. Understanding the basic elements of your birth chart is crucial before we jump into learning about relationship astrology specifically. Think of this section as your glossary, which you can easily refer back to throughout the rest of the book in order to better understand your specific placements. On page xvi, you'll find my birth chart, for reference. Now, let's look at how you can create yours.

How to pull up your birth chart

1. **HAVE YOUR EXACT TIME, PLACE, AND CITY OF BIRTH AT HAND.** To pull up your birth chart online, you'll need to input information into an astrology website, including your exact time, place, and city of birth. I recommend using the free websites astro.com or astro-seek.com. On astro.com's home page, click on the section titled "Charts and Calculations" and then "Extended Chart Selection." If you are using astro-seek.com, go to the top-left drop-down menu that says, "Free Horoscopes, Charts, Calculations" and select "Birth Natal Chart Online Calculator." From there, enter your exact time, place, and city of birth. Unfortunately, approximate birth times will lead to misleading results; even if the birth time is thirty minutes off, it can drastically shift where the planets fall in your chart. If there is no way to find your time of birth (either from talking to family members or getting in touch with the hospital at which you were born), you can always work with an astrologer to determine what it might be.

2. **CHOOSE A HOUSE SYSTEM.** Before you calculate your chart on either website, there is an option to change your house system. (I will get into what the houses are later on in this chapter, so don't worry about that terminology at this moment.) There are various house systems that astrologers use, and no one way of dividing out the houses is better than another. The default house system on most websites is Placidus, but I use whole sign houses in my practice (see page 15), as it has proven to be the most effective when I am studying charts and giving readings to people. Therefore, to best follow along in this book, you will want to switch your house system to whole sign. On both astro.com and astro-seek.com, there is a drop-down menu on the same page where you enter in your birth information labelled "house system." From the drop-down menu, select the system simply labelled "whole sign."

3. **CALCULATE YOUR CHART.** Now that everything is ready to go, simply click "Calculate your Chart" or "Show the Chart." You should be met with a circular diagram that looks similar to the example chart I gave on page xvi.

Before we move on, I really recommend taking the time now to pull up your birth chart. It's going to help you get the most out of this book as you read and will allow you to understand how each section relates to you personally.

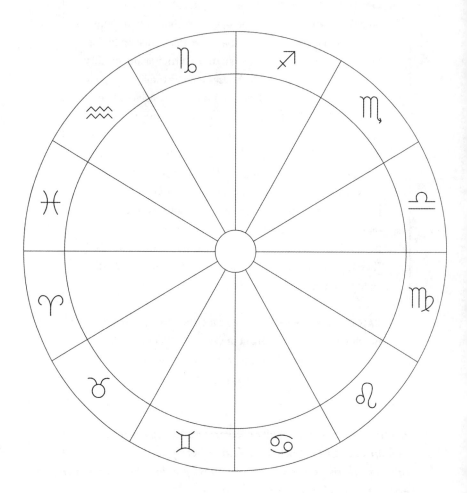

The 12 signs positioned around a birth chart.

CHAPTER 1

The First Step: The Signs

When you're reading your weekly horoscope or sharing a funny astrology meme or online article, you're usually looking at your sun sign, which has come to be known as simply your "sign." However, everyone actually has all 12 signs in their chart. Read through the information below to familiarize yourself with the traits of all 12 signs. Based on your own chart, you will express the qualities of these signs in different ways.

ARIES: As the first sign in the zodiac, Aries likes to initiate and set ideas into motion. It's a sign that makes quick decisions and is very decisive about what it wants. Aries doesn't like to sit around and let life happen—it wants to be part of the action. Because Aries is always thinking about what's next, it can often grow restless if plans are slow to form or other people aren't up to the same speed. The challenges for this sign are that it can be a bit too self-focused or selfish and lack sensitivity to the feelings of other people. Aries has also been known to have a bit of a temper and sometimes acts on impulse, reacting immediately without reflecting first. At its best, though, Aries is inspiring and takes the risks most other people aren't brave enough to go for. This gives the sign of Aries incredible charisma and strong leadership potential.

TAURUS: Taurus is the sign that tends to be the most patient and grounded. It has the ability to keep at whatever goal it's pursuing over an extended period of time without giving up. When committing to an opportunity or relationship, Taurus will put a lot of deliberate thought into something before making a decision. Taurus also appreciates the beauty in life and likes to engage in calming activities that involve the physical body, whether that be walks in nature, cooking, doing yoga, or engaging in any other activity that involves the hands. The major criticism Taurus faces is that it can be slow, stubborn, or too set in its own ways. It also gets the reputation for being too materialistic, but Taurus is just very sensitive to how everything looks, feels, and smells around them. It is a sign that appreciates high quality and creativity, and it also has a love for comfort and pleasure.

GEMINI: Gemini is the sign associated with the mind and communication, so it needs a lot of mental stimulation. Gemini enjoys reading, writing, podcasting, and finding other ways to connect with people and trade ideas. This sign is very curious and may know a bit about a variety of different topics. Its infinite knowledge comes in handy when navigating social situations and making small talk with people. Gemini usually knows how to ask the right questions. The biggest challenge this sign faces is that it is too flaky and all over the place. There is often trouble committing to just one decision or one relationship, because something new is always right around the corner, piquing its interest. However, it is Gemini's go-with-the-flow attitude that makes it so easily adaptable to change. If Gemini is put in an unfamiliar situation, it can adapt and pick up new information quickly.

CANCER: Cancer is the nurturer of the zodiac. This sign tends to be very protective over the people it cares about, and it can take a while for it to fully open up to new people. Cancer wants to build a nurturing home life for itself, and it's a sign that favors deeper connections and enjoys taking care of friends and loved ones. Cancer also has strong ties to the home and family, so where Cancer falls in your chart will give clues into your specific home situation and your attitude toward family. This sign often falls under criticism for being too sensitive and moody, though, and its emotions may fluctuate quite a bit. But it's these same traits that make Cancer a good confidant, as it can easily empathize and offer advice to other people. In addition, Cancer has an affinity for the past, so there is often an interest in history, family ancestry, or even vintage items.

LEO: Leo needs to be able to shine in some area of life. It is a sign that has a very warm and playful spirit and is often full of creative ideas. Leo thrives when it has an outlet for self-expression, such as an artistic hobby or pursuing design, fashion, or performance. It may also have a strong connection with children, and, in addition, Leo holds on to a childlike sense of wonder and enthusiasm no matter its age. However, this sign is often associated with being overly dramatic and bossy. Leo also craves attention and validation but must learn to give these things to itself. In addition, this sign can be rather shy and hyperaware of how it's seen by other people, but this often means it has a great sense of style since so much focus is on appearance. Despite Leo's self-centered tendencies, it's still a fiercely loyal sign and will also be very blunt and honest with people.

VIRGO: Virgo is an expert in handling everyday, practical details. This sign enjoys being productive and of service to others, and it's always looking for ways to improve upon itself or be more efficient in its daily routines. It also craves cleanliness and order and has a very analytical way of looking at the world. Virgo is very into wellness practices, so tends to prioritize regular exercise, eating healthily, and finding the perfect skincare routine. However, Virgo can often get fixated on every little imperfection and become overly critical of both itself and others. There is a lot of pressure to be perfect or try to fix everyone else's problems, and it may be difficult for Virgo to sit still and just be. Virgo's perfectionist nature is not all bad, though, and this sign is usually great with juggling facts and numbers, catching spelling errors, and doing any type of activity that involves writing or communication.

LIBRA: Libra is the sign associated with partnerships; it is always considering the thoughts and opinions of others. Rather than mingling in huge group settings, Libra values spending quality time with the people it's closest to. It is through Libra's interactions with other people that it is able to gain a greater sense of self. Libra makes a big effort to maintain peace and balance in all relationships, but it can also mean that this sign is pretty indecisive out of a fear of upsetting anyone. Libra is quick to shy away from conflict and confrontation, but at the same time it's very aware of what is polite and constitutes good social conduct. In addition, Libra has a particular aesthetic, and typically a love for art, fashion, and travel. Keen on always obtaining more knowledge, Libra loves exchanging ideas and information with people, and weighing their opinions against those of someone else.

SCORPIO: Scorpio craves emotional depth and intimacy but often has difficulty sharing this side with others. There is a need to control its feelings, and it takes a lot for this sign to open up and be vulnerable with someone. A very intuitive sign, Scorpio is quickly able to pick up on who a person really is and often enjoys hearing about other people's problems and analyzing them. There is usually an interest in psychology, sexuality, topics pertaining to life and death, or the occult. Scorpio likes learning about everything that is hidden and not readily discussed, and this sign goes through regular cycles of inner transformation, where one part of itself is shed in order to make way for a new sense of self. Scorpio frequently comes under fire for having an obsessive and sometimes controlling personality, but it is this same intensity that can lead to it being an expert in a particular field of interest.

SAGITTARIUS: Sagittarius is the world traveler of the zodiac. This sign loves seeking out new adventures and pushing itself out of its comfort zone. Travel is a big activity for Sagittarius, but it doesn't want to just visit places as a tourist and would rather fully immerse itself in another country and their traditions. Sagittarius loves learning about various cultures, beliefs, and spiritualities, and it will either go back to school to pursue a higher degree or continue to do a lot of research and writing in its own time. However, it may sometimes get criticized for being too opinionated or quick to brush off another person's point of view. In addition, this sign's enthusiasm and optimistic spirit can sometimes get itself into situations where it has taken on too much work and can't deliver on what was promised. No matter what type of difficulty Sagittarius encounters, though, it usually views every experience as a necessary lesson and opportunity for growth.

CAPRICORN: Capricorn is extremely ambitious and aspires to be respected and admired in its particular field. No stranger to hard work, this sign typically has a five-year plan for the future and knows exactly what steps need to be taken to get to where it wants to be. It also doesn't take commitment lightly, and only agrees to situations and relationships if it sees long-term potential there. Capricorn is a fan of tradition and following what has been proven to work in the past, but it can often get hung up on needing too many credentials before taking a risk, or not feeling good enough in comparison to other people. More often than not, it is Capricorn's self-imposed restrictions that end up holding it back. This is a sign that comes into itself as it gets older, so any difficulty Capricorn may have with relationships, sharing emotions or figuring out what life path is best will get easier with age.

AQUARIUS: Aquarius is a sign that is independent and needs to have a lot of freedom and space. It is usually two steps ahead of everyone else and concerned with what comes next. Aquarius has an inventive way of thinking and comes up with radical new concepts and ideas that can help serve a greater good. This sign doesn't like to follow trends or copy whatever everyone else is doing and will often choose to be different and challenge the status quo. Though Aquarius knows a wide network of people and is quite social, it can still have a lingering feeling of being an outsider or not completely understood. Aquarius may sometimes get criticized for being aloof, unemotional, or too rebellious. Though it may come across as a bit detached, it's simply because this sign is always in its head, brainstorming ways in which it can implement changes or take the risks no one else dares to try.

PISCES: Pisces is very sensitive and intuitive, often picking up on how other people are feeling as well as the subtle energy circulating in its environment. Carving out time to be alone is necessary for Pisces because it may frequently become overwhelmed by feelings. This sign is also very compassionate and giving but can sometimes lack boundaries and end up putting too much effort into people who don't deserve it. Pisces also has escapist tendencies, but only because it yearns for a connection to something bigger than itself. Instead of trying to dissociate from their feelings, Pisces may find greater inner peace through spiritually oriented activities like learning astrology, developing a regular meditation practice, or getting involved in community service. Exploring matters pertaining to mental health, finding time for creative hobbies, or simply daydreaming are also other outlets that this sign enjoys.

Different Ways of Looking at the Signs

AS YOU WENT through each of the 12 signs, you may have noticed that a few different signs shared some common traits. Sagittarius and Aries are both very action-oriented, while Scorpio and Taurus don't easily give up when faced with a challenge. Taking the signs one step further, we can categorize each one according to its modality and element. The sign elements include fire, earth, air, and water, and there are three signs in each element. Signs that are of the same element share a like-minded temperament and tend to have a similar way of expressing themselves. Meanwhile, the sign modalities are cardinal, fixed, and mutable. There are four signs in each modality, one from each element. Signs of the same modality react to life similarly, and they also share a like-minded approach to work, responsibility, and problem solving.

The different modalities and elements will become very important when we look at relationship compatibility, because you are more likely to attract people who share signs of the same element or modality as you. We will dive deeper into the relationship dynamics later, but for now check to see if you have a significant number of planets (the glyphs located within your chart) in a particular sign, element, or modality more than another.

YOUR UNIQUE SELF-EXPRESSION: SIGN ELEMENTS

FIRE: ARIES, LEO, SAGITTARIUS

Fire signs need frequent action and excitement in their lives, and they are sure of what they want and how they're going to get there. Fire signs are also very passionate about their specific interests, and they like to take risks and jump into new experiences immediately, without worrying about the small details. They usually have an enthusiasm that draws other people to them, but they can easily grow restless and impatient.

EARTH SIGNS: TAURUS, VIRGO, CAPRICORN

Earth signs are hard workers, and they like to have a set routine or laid-out vision for their future. They also tend to be more concerned with the practical details of everyday life, and they usually need to plan ahead before jumping into anything too quickly. Earth signs are also very reliable and can be counted on to show up when they say they will. They're good with managing various responsibilities.

AIR SIGNS: GEMINI, LIBRA, AQUARIUS

Air signs are the big thinkers, and their minds are usually running a million miles a minute. They often have many ideas that they are keen to share with others and can easily take in a lot of information at once. Air signs are usually interested in work or hobbies that involve communication, whether that be writing, teaching, making videos, podcasting, or having a big online presence.

WATER SIGNS: CANCER, SCORPIO, PISCES

Water signs tend to have strong intuitive qualities; they're very aware of people's emotions and the energy around them. They're usually good at listening to problems and offering helpful advice, and they feel things very deeply. Because of this, they may get very attached to both people or places, often reflecting on their own emotions or behavioral patterns.

HOW YOU GO AFTER WHAT YOU WANT: SIGN MODALITIES

CARDINAL: ARIES, CANCER, LIBRA, CAPRICORN

Cardinal signs like to initiate and create. These are the signs that are self-starters and can get an idea off the ground and running. They may also be a bit restless and need to remain constantly active, so these signs might not always stick around to see their vision through until the end. No matter where you live in the world, you can associate the cardinal signs with the start of new seasons. In the northern hemisphere Aries is the beginning of spring, Cancer is summer, Libra is autumn, and Capricorn is winter. If you're in the southern hemisphere, the seasons are reversed.

FIXED: TAURUS, LEO, SCORPIO, AQUARIUS

Fixed signs mark the middle of each season, so you can think of them as sustaining whatever has already been started. When these signs are interested in something, they usually have an intense determination to find out all there is to know and can sometimes have an obsessive personality. They don't easily give up and will keep at a particular task or relationship until a conclusion is reached. Fixed signs also like to be in control and aren't often great with change unless it is instigated by them.

MUTABLE: GEMINI, VIRGO, SAGITTARIUS, PISCES

Mutable signs like to go with the flow. They mark the end of seasons, so they embody transitional periods. These signs can easily adapt to change, and they remain flexible and open-minded about what's to come. They're good at taking the ideas or projects others have started and either reframing them or seeing them through. However, they can also be a bit wishy-washy when it comes to making decisions—it may just take them a while to commit. They're known for changing their minds frequently and don't want to be roped into making a final decision until it is absolutely necessary.

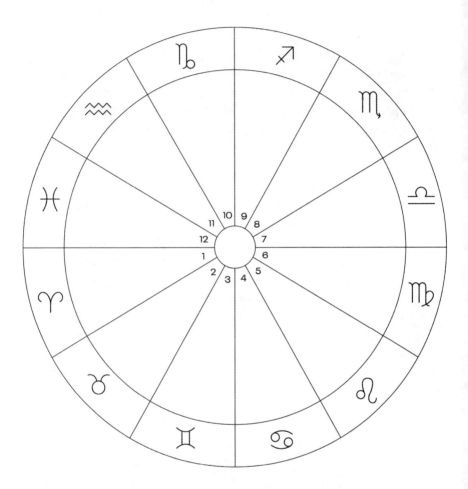

The houses are numbered in a counterclockwise direction.
One house, one sign.

CHAPTER 2

Where the Action Unfolds: The Houses

Now that we've familiarized ourselves with all the signs, let's get into the houses that comprise your birth chart. The entire 360-degree circle that is your chart is divided into 12 different sections, which resemble pie slices. If you look at the diagram opposite, you'll see how the different sections are now numbered 1–12. Each of these sections is a house, and each house corresponds to a very specific area of life. There are houses that point to work and career, while others symbolize relationships, family, or health, among many other different topics.

As I mentioned earlier, I use whole sign houses in my practice. With the whole sign house system, every house is 30 degrees and corresponds with exactly one sign of the zodiac. Starting with house one, which is the house that contains your rising sign (also known as your ascendant), every house moving forward (counterclockwise) is then associated with the subsequent sign in the order of the zodiac. For example, the chart opposite has an Aries ascendant, so you can see that house one is Aries, house two is Taurus, house three is Gemini, house four is Cancer, and so on.

When you go through the meanings of each house detailed in this chapter, you can also start to blend the traits of each sign with the house it is associated with—or that it "rules"—in your birth chart. Going back to the Aries rising example from page 15, when you're reading about the first house you can also apply Aries-type traits to that house, while you can blend Taurus qualities with the meaning of the second house and Gemini characteristics with the third house. You may also notice that in your chart there are some houses that are occupied with more planetary glyphs than others. If there is a house that contains a lot of planets, or even one or two, then that area will be emphasized throughout the course of your life and there may be many lessons to learn there. On the other hand, if there is a house that contains no glyphs, it doesn't mean that house is "empty," because there is still a sign that is found on the border of that house.

Take a moment now to look at your chart. Even if there are houses that don't have planets in them, you will still want to familiarize yourself with the meanings of all 12 houses below.

FIRST HOUSE: You can think of the first house as your literal self. It embodies your appearance, your personal style, and also your physical body. The first house is the same sign as your rising sign, or ascendant, so this is the part of the chart that informs how you approach new situations and what first impression you give. It also indicates your general approach to life and what type of traits you lean into when developing a greater sense of self. For example, a Leo first house (or Leo rising) would inject a sense of creativity into everything that they do, while a Capricorn first house (or Capricorn rising) would always have a sense of duty and responsibility that they carry into the rest of their lives.

SECOND HOUSE: The second house is one of three houses in your chart that is associated with work, but it specifically has to do with money and the unique skills you bring to your job. This house often involves starting businesses and entrepreneurial skills, so it can indicate whether you are someone who wants to work for themselves, as well as how much confidence you have in asserting ideas at your job and asking for what you deserve. Additionally, the second house has to do with spending habits, what you like splurging on and how well you handle your money. The house is also concerned with your values; it encompasses what you deem worthy of buying, as well as what motivates you to put in effort at work.

THIRD HOUSE: The third house is one of several social and relationship-oriented houses in your chart: it pertains to everyday communication. It's about taking the bigger knowledge or abstract ideas you may have and breaking them down in a way that is easy for other people to understand. This house often concerns practical information like online articles, social media content, and podcasts. It's also about how you process information, voice your opinions, and go about your day-to-day errands. The third house often speaks to your interactions with nearby acquaintances and neighbors, as well as siblings, if applicable, and the type of relationship you have with these people in your life. In addition, this house pertains to travel, but more of the shorter, long-weekend-away or day-trip variety.

FOURTH HOUSE: The fourth house is the lowest part of the chart, so it makes sense that it concerns the core foundation of your life. This house explains the environment at home during your childhood, as well as how you perceive the relationship you have with your family. The fourth house can also pertain more specifically with your mother or maternal figure, as well as your ancestry and the past. Additionally, it is concerned with your innermost emotions and how you express them. Your living habits fall under the fourth, too—this house explains why some people do well with housemates while others desperately need their own space. Anything pertaining to moving, home renovations, or decorating your domestic space will also fall into the realm of the fourth.

FIFTH HOUSE: Creativity, self-expression, and self-confidence all feature prominently as fifth house themes. This part of the chart has to do with the hobbies you pursue in your own time for fun. Most recreational activities fall into the fifth, such as going on vacation, playing games, or getting involved in some type of performance art or other artistic endeavor. Children and pregnancy fall into the fifth house as well, so it can explain your attitude toward having kids as well as tapping into your own inner child. The fifth house is another house that pertains to relationships, but it mostly encompasses casual dating, flirting, and sexual preferences. Oftentimes this house will also be about finding greater self-esteem when you're around other people and knowing your worth in romantic situations.

SIXTH HOUSE: The sixth is another house that has to do with work, but more specifically the smaller, more mundane tasks you do at your job on an everyday basis. It also pertains to co-workers or the work you do for other people—service industry jobs or work that involves dealing immediately with another person fall into the sixth. This house is also about your daily routines and rituals, and how productive you are. It can explain why some people need a structured nine-to-five job, while others may prefer to work at random hours of the day. In addition, the sixth house encompasses your physical health. Any food sensitivities, injuries, or other bodily concerns are sixth house themes, as well as exercise, eating habits, and other wellness practices.

SEVENTH HOUSE: The seventh house is the number one house to look at when understanding relationships. This house has to do with one-on-one partnerships, both platonic and romantic. Where the fifth house is more about the dating process, the seventh points to a relationship that is more established and committed. This house describes what type of traits you may look for in a romantic partner, as well as what parts of yourself you may end up projecting onto other people. Often, traits associated with the seventh house in your chart lie dormant within yourself, and it takes a close relationship coming into your life to awaken that side of you. The seventh is also concerned with formal business partnerships or other types of close relationships in your life, like a best friend or confidant.

EIGHTH HOUSE: The eighth house builds upon seventh house themes: it is concerned with taking partnerships to the next level by merging your life with someone else's. The eighth has to do with splitting finances with a partner or receiving an inheritance or financial support from someone. It could also be money made from investments or other types of passive income. Aside from money, the eighth house deals with themes related to death and rebirth. This may include experiencing loss, either through a break-up or someone close to you dying, or it could mean periodically shedding parts of yourself that no longer serve you. In addition, the eighth is related to therapy and better understanding your own behavioral patterns. No topic is off limits with this house, so people with many planets placed here will often enjoy discussing sex, death, money, or the occult. Finally, the eighth house has to do with the deeper side of sex and relationships, where you feel like you're fully merging with someone and being emotionally vulnerable. This is the house that can either make or break a partnership.

NINTH HOUSE: After the heaviness of the eighth, the ninth comes with a sense of optimism and freedom. This house has to do with broadening your horizons and seeing more of the world. It deals with foreign cultures, languages, and international travel. The ninth is also about higher education, so it specifically pertains to college or getting a degree beyond that. Outside of school, the ninth encompasses the learning you do on your own time as well, so any intensive research or online courses and workshops on a specific topic will fall into this part of the chart. Furthermore, the ninth house contains writing and publishing, as well as philosophy, spirituality, and religion. For instance, astrology falls into this house. Whereas the third house is about everyday communications, the ninth house is for pondering more abstract and bigger picture topics.

TENTH HOUSE: The third and final house that encompasses work is the tenth. This house is the highest point of the chart, and it represents long-term career ambitions and your life calling. It's not so much about the tasks you do on a daily basis, but more to do with where you see yourself in the future with your career and what bigger goals you want to be working toward. In addition, the tenth house has to do with your public image, as well as any leadership position where you're being seen by other people. When you look at a celebrity or someone on social media, the traits associated with their tenth house are telling—even more so than their rising sign. Finally, the tenth can be associated with the father or father figure and describes the type of relationship you have with him.

ELEVENTH HOUSE: The eleventh is another social part of the chart: it encompasses the bigger groups of people you associate with. Any type of community activity or cause that you're passionate about falls into this house, as well as networking and branching out of your usual circle of people. The eleventh also describes your approach to friendships and can be very telling of whether you're someone who keeps in touch with childhood friends, or if you're someone who likes to jump around between groups. In addition, this house speaks to the people who support you and can sometimes be your audience if you're someone who works for yourself or publicly promotes your work. Finally, the eleventh has to do with your hopes and dreams for the future and the visions that you want to make into a reality.

TWELFTH HOUSE: The final house in your chart, the twelfth concerns solitude and letting go. Endings fall into the realm of the twelfth house, so it's often about learning how to release control over a particular situation or experiencing loss through a break-up or death. This house is also associated with mental health, illness, and hospitals, and it embodies repressed emotions and fears that may come up from time to time. In addition, the twelfth has to do with the ways in which you work against yourself, so any self-sabotaging behaviors. It can also represent hidden enemies and people not being who you thought they were. On a more positive note, the twelfth house pertains to community service and doing work for the greater good. Various spiritual activities are associated with the twelfth, such as meditation, manifestation, and better understanding your subconscious patterns.

There are four angles in your chart.

CHAPTER 3

Critical Areas of Life: The Angles

We've covered signs and houses, now it's time to add in the four angles. These are the ascendant (AC), descendant (DC), Midheaven (MC), and *Imum Coeli* (IC). These pertain to self, relationships, career, and home respectively. Each of these angles is found in a particular house of your chart and represents one of the four main pillars of your life. On astro.com, the descendant and *Imum Coeli* aren't labelled, but they can always be found exactly opposite the ascendant and Midheaven respectively.

Angles can feel like an added complication, but I want to stress their importance because they become crucial when looking at relationship compatibility and also determining the timing of romantic activity. We'll look at your descendant and ascendant more in Part Two but, for now, here's an introduction to what each of the angles signify.

Take a look at where your angles sit in your chart and use the below to see how their influence might be showing up in your life.

THE ASCENDANT (AC): This angle, which is also referred to as your rising sign, is always found in the first house of your chart. Similar to the description of the first house, the ascendant is the lens through which you perceive the world. It also describes how you present yourself and how others see you. The sign in which your ascendant falls colors how you approach unfamiliar situations, as well as the other various areas of your life.

THE DESCENDANT (DC): The descendant can always be found exactly opposite the ascendant and is marked at the same degree, just in the opposing sign in your seventh house. Whereas you may easily embody the traits of your ascendant, the descendant often indicates the traits that lie dormant within you. You may end up projecting some of these traits onto a partner or find that you are better able to understand and express this side of yourself through close one-on-one relationships.

THE MIDHEAVEN (MC): The Midheaven is the most visible part of your chart and describes what type of public image you give off. Similar to the tenth house, the Midheaven describes your life calling, as well what long-term career aspirations would be the most fulfilling. Using whole sign houses, the MC is typically found in the ninth, tenth, or eleventh houses of the chart, and, in rare cases, the twelfth or eighth houses. Whatever house and sign the Midheaven is located in for you will tell you more about what career you would be happiest in. For example, a ninth house Midheaven would incorporate ninth house themes like writing, teaching, or foreign travel into their work, while an eleventh house Midheaven may like to engage in group activities or collaborate with friends in their career.

THE IMUM COELI (IC): The IC can be found exactly opposite the MC, at the same degree in the opposing sign. Using whole sign houses, the IC is usually located in the third, fourth, or fifth houses or, in rare cases, the second or sixth houses. Depending on what house and sign your IC falls into will give clues into your home life and family relationships. For example, a fifth house IC may mean that you grew up in a creative or playful type family, while a third house IC means you may feel most at home when on the road, traveling, or that your siblings play a huge role in your life. The IC also indicates early-life conditioning, your ancestry, and what you need to feel safe and secure. This angle is a very private part of yourself that not many people know about.

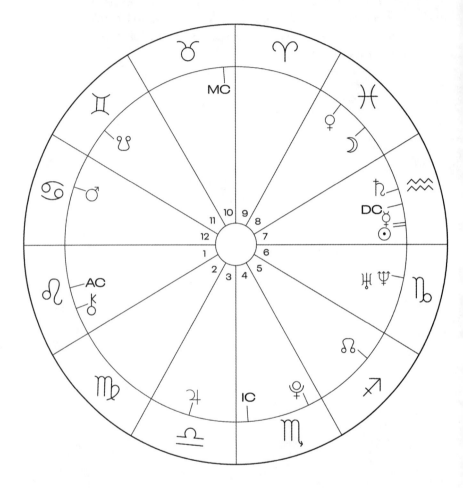

Planets are symbolized by the glyphs in the chart above.

CHAPTER 4

The Main Characters: The Planets

Now that we've learned about the signs, houses, and angles, we can move on to the planets. In the diagram opposite, you can see that the planets are represented by the glyphs placed within the chart. You can think of them as the cast of characters in your chart—each planet has specific traits they bring to both a sign and a house.

The sign that the planets are placed in shows how they express themselves, while the house they are found in indicates what area of life they put their energy into, as well as what activities they influence. For example, let's say you have Venus (love language, personal tastes) in the sign of Scorpio (obsessive, craves intensity, wants to go in depth) in the third house (daily communication and practical information). Therefore, you may enjoy writing or speaking about emotionally charged topics like psychology and sexuality, or you may need a romantic partner with whom you can openly and easily discuss these types of things.

Here's an introduction to each of the planets and luminaries. As with the houses and signs, it's important to get a firm understanding of the character of each one. Read through the information below and don't worry if it takes some time to get your head around them—you'll get the hang of it.

The Luminaries
and Inner Planets

SUN: The sun is what you immediately think of when someone asks what sign you are. It embodies your core identity and sense of self. The sun also represents the traits that you continue to grow into over the course of your life; it is who you are learning how to be. Finally, the sun represents your vitality, and it also informs what types of goals and interests you want to pursue.

MOON: The moon is your innermost self; it describes how you process and express your emotions. It also indicates your instinctual emotional reactions that you may have picked up in childhood, as well as the relationship you have with your mother or maternal figure. Finally, the moon represents your approach to intimate relationships, as well as your self-care routines and at-home habits.

MERCURY: Mercury describes your communication style, such as how you think and process new information or the way in which you convey your ideas and opinions to other people. It can also describe your particular sense of humor, as well as what you're interested in reading, writing, or talking about.

VENUS: Venus describes who and what you're attracted to, your style of relating to others, and how you express love and affection. It encompasses your approach toward both romantic relationships as well as friendships. This planet also has to do with your personal taste, such as what music you're into, your style, and anything else you deem to be aesthetically pleasing. In addition to the second house, Venus also points to your spending habits and what you like to splurge on.

MARS: Mars shows your style of handling conflict and how you process feelings of anger and frustration. It indicates how you act on your specific goals and desires, as well as what activities you enjoy putting your energy into. Mars also reveals how direct or indirect you might be. In the realm of relationships, this planet signals your attitude toward sex and what turns you on.

Social Planets and Outer Planets

JUPITER: Jupiter is indicative of optimism and growth. Wherever Jupiter is located in your chart is an area where opportunities may come easily, or where you have a lot of faith that will naturally work out. However, Jupiter also shows what talents you may take for granted, or where you may overdo it in life, whether that be spending too much money, taking on too much work, or giving all of yourself away in a relationship. In addition, Jupiter can also represent foreign cultures, what you enjoy learning about, or where you may encounter important teachers or mentors.

SATURN: Saturn is a planet that is associated with hardship and restriction, and it often indicates where you may feel a big sense of duty or stress. This planet usually represents an area where you may encounter much fear or anxiety, or where you constantly come up against limitations or self-imposed restrictions. Saturn is not all bad though, and it will show what topic or area of life you can eventually gain a mastery of, usually through repeated lessons and over an extended period of time. Saturn ripens with age, so the area it's activating in your chart often becomes easier as you get older.

URANUS: With Uranus, expect the unexpected. This planet represents sudden change and disruption, and it often brings an unpredictable type of energy to wherever it is placed in your chart. Uranus isn't necessarily thought of as good or bad—it simply shakes things up. In addition, this planet has to do with breaking free from restrictions, not liking to be controlled, and challenging the status quo. It indicates an area where you may go against the grain or where you may need a lot of freedom to do your own thing. Finally, Uranus can stand for technology or even electricity.

NEPTUNE: Neptune indicates things that aren't entirely what they seem to be. Depending on its chart placement, this planet often blurs the reality of a situation, making it hard to set boundaries or get a clear picture of that area of life. With Neptune, you have to become comfortable with the lack of structure or the inability to always find answers. There is usually a desire to connect to something bigger than yourself in the area of life that Neptune affects, or its placement shows where you may need to lean into creativity and the arts. Neptune can also represent film, photography, fantasy, and mysticism.

PLUTO: Pluto symbolizes deep inner transformation and can often bring about themes of loss followed by rebirth in the part of your chart where it is located. Pluto is telling of where you may encounter the most power struggles in your life, as well as where you're learning how to face hidden parts of yourself. Pluto urges you to release your need to always be in control.

Other Important Chart Elements

THE NORTH AND SOUTH NODES: The Nodes are not planets, but rather mathematical points on the chart. The Nodes always fall between a pair of signs that are oposite to one another, and they also indicate the signs in which solar and lunar eclipses were taking place the year you were born. The North Node points to activities in which you may feel the most fulfilled or engaged, as well as what traits you are meant to develop throughout your life. If you're feeling confused about your life path, check to see if you're following the qualities represented by the sign and house placement of your North Node. Meanwhile, the South Node represents abilities you already possess and can easily tap into. However, the South Node can act like a security blanket: there is usually a need to move away from the activities or areas of life it symbolizes or rely less heavily on them. On astro.com, the South Node will not automatically appear, so under "Display and Calculation Options" on the birth data entry page, you will want to check "descending node."

CHIRON: Chiron is a minor planet that is sometimes called the "wounded healer." It often points to an area where you may be vulnerable or insecure, and also where you feel like you're lacking something. In the part of your chart that Chiron activates, there could be a fear of inhabiting your full self. However, Chiron also shows where you have the most capacity to heal over time and, in turn, help other people with similar experiences.

Now that we've gone over the signs, houses, angles, and planets, you should have a good grasp of the basic tools for reading your birth chart. Don't worry about the lines running through the middle of your chart for now. These are called aspects, and we'll discuss them in detail in Part Two. For now, let's move on to do a deep dive into three of the most important planets relating to your relationships. These are your moon, Venus, and Mars signs. Learning about these three planets in my own chart was what really made astrology begin to click for me.

Gaining Greater Self-Acceptance: Understanding Your Birth Chart through the Lens of Relationships

When I first started learning about astrology, I pulled up my birth chart online and went through every single planet. I googled what they all meant, and I read every single interpretation that I could find. I understood my sun sign to be Aquarius, but reading about my Pisces moon and Venus, my Mars in Cancer, and my Saturn in the seventh house is what got me officially hooked on astrology.

I felt like someone had explained my personality entirely. Before this moment I had spent years reading about what it was like to be an Aquarius sun, but I didn't feel like it fully encapsulated me. I was never aloof or detached when it came to relationships—I was actually the exact opposite. I would get attached to people very quickly, even if I didn't know them that well, and then would spend months fantasizing about what could have been long after the fling had ended. This is why it is important to explore the other elements of your birth chart, beyond just your "sign," because astrology can explain the many facets of your personality.

As I explored the various elements of my birth chart, I felt so validated in all areas of my life, but especially when it came to dating and relationships. Instead of trying to reject certain parts of my personality or take on the interests of someone else just so that they would like me, I was able to fully accept myself and recognize what I desired from a relationship. In this section, you will be learning how to decipher all of this information in your own chart. First, we will take a closer look at your moon, Venus, and Mars signs. If, up until this point, you have only known your "sign," these chapters may bring up a lot of aha moments. Next, you will be introduced to aspects, so you can understand how these three planets interact with the other planets in your chart. Then, we will move on to cover the relationship-oriented houses, adding yet another layer of interpretation to how you approach dating and relationships in general. Finally, for those of you feeling hopeless when it comes to your love life, we will look at the chart configurations that could be making you feel this way, learning how no one is ever doomed in love. The following chapters will serve to bring your attention back to yourself and what you really want. Before we can learn about what it means to have astrological compatibility, you have to first learn how to make yourself happy and fulfilled.

CHAPTER 5

Discovering Your Inner Self: The Moon

Now that we have a firm grasp on the basics of your birth chart, let's focus on the planets that specifically pertain to relationships, dating, and intimacy: the moon, Venus, and Mars. While we'll mainly be looking at how these planets show up in romantic partnerships, the following information can also be applied to your family relationships or close friendships.

The signs in which the moon, Venus, and Mars fall in your chart will shed some light on how you express yourself, whether you're in the early stages of dating someone, already in a long-term relationship, or single and just want to better understand yourself and why you're drawn to certain types of people. Before we can combine all parts of the chart together as a whole, let's take a look at each of these planets on their own.

The moon represents:

- How you express your emotions
- The ways in which you approach intimacy
- How easy or difficult it is to get emotionally close to people
- The style in which you nurture both yourself and others
- How you experienced your early home environment and the relationship with your family
- What home means to you as an adult
- What type of self-care rituals are the most fitting for you

I want to talk about the moon first, because it is the single most important planet when it comes to building intimacy and feeling nurtured by someone. Unlike the sun sign (which can be determined simply by knowing which month you were born), an exact birth time, date, and year is needed to calculate your moon sign. The moon changes signs about every two and a half days, making it a planet that is uniquely personal to you. The moon functions differently from sign to sign, and knowing your moon placement will help you understand what you want and need most out of a close relationship.

To start, the moon embodies traits that are less obvious to everyone else. If the sun and rising signs point to what others might immediately see in you, the moon is the part of your personality that tends to be a bit more hidden. Think of the moon as your inner self, the side that tends to come out only in your super close relationships.

Oftentimes, the moon's placement will reveal something about your early home environment and the behaviors that you picked up in childhood that you may revert to. It is very indicative of your immediate, emotional reactions when someone upsets you or you find yourself in an unfamiliar and uncomfortable situation. It doesn't always mean that these are the most mature behaviors, and frequently the moon shows patterns that need to be rewired as an adult. For instance, if someone were to disagree with you and you were upset about it, your reaction would differ based on your moon sign. An Aries moon may respond impulsively and get pretty heated, while a Capricorn moon may be a lot more reserved about what feelings they reveal to people. By understanding your moon, you can become more aware of how you share your feelings in your relationships and how you might be able to improve upon this. Once I fully understood the traits associated with my own Pisces moon, I realized that I was a very sensitive person and tended to take on other people's problems and try to fix them, especially those of my romantic partners. I had not been aware that I did this, so now I make more of a conscious effort to check in, set boundaries, and make sure I'm taking care of myself first.

In addition, the moon tends to hint at the personality traits of your mother or maternal figure and how you perceive the relationship with her to be. Because of its close ties to the home, the moon sign will therefore show what qualities you may seek in a long-term partner, with whom you plan to build a home and a family. It points to what you need in a relationship to feel nurtured, comfortable, and secure.

However, you can't rely entirely on your partner to provide you with these things, so it's important to tap into your moon sign for clues on how to feel more secure and fulfilled. If your moon is being suppressed or ignored, you won't feel completely happy, and it could feel as if there's a void that you're constantly trying to fill. You may search for your moon sign traits in other people, but the key is learning how to nurture yourself and your moon first. By establishing little rituals and self-care habits that are in line with what your moon craves, you can in turn attract better relationships.

Once you've located in which sign the moon falls in your birth chart, check the description of that sign in this chapter. It may also be enlightening to read up on the moon sign of a partner, best friend, or family member.

ARIES MOON

If you have an Aries moon, you have an inner restlessness that pushes you to take action. You might be someone who likes to remain upbeat and positive, and you're always looking ahead to what's next. You have a lot of passion and enthusiasm, and other people tend to be drawn to your uplifting spirit. Because you radiate so much energy, you're constantly pushing yourself to take risks, try out new experiences, or create something of your own. When expressing your feelings, though, you can be pretty direct and blunt. You may also lose patience easily—when you've decided you want something, you want it now, in that very moment. This behavior can come off as demanding or rude to some people, but at the end of the day, you just know what you desire and you aren't afraid to go after it. It's these same qualities that make you a successful leader, as well as someone who doesn't back down from a challenge.

When dating, you may find it frustrating to sit back and let someone else come to you. You may often be the pursuer, as you tend to be braver than most in reaching out and making the first move or sending that initial text. You might want to be wary, though, of turning up the heat too quickly with the people you date. You could end up in romantic situations that develop fast, only to see them end just as abruptly. It may be helpful to slow down and get to know someone before rushing into anything or making impulsive decisions. On the other hand, you might be quick to move on if you don't feel an immediate spark with someone. You're looking for passion in your relationships, so it's easy to tell when that just isn't there.

As an Aries moon, you're also comfortable putting yourself first. You know how necessary it is to prioritize your own needs and interests, but, at the same time, it might be challenging for you to step back and consider how someone else might be feeling. You could quickly brush off other people's problems, and you may not like talking about sad emotions or break-ups. Additionally, when you feel passionately about something, you may react impulsively in the heat of the moment. You get worked up pretty quickly, but often only a few hours later you've forgotten what upset you in the first place. Though you're not someone who holds a grudge, developing greater empathy and patience with people is still an area you may need to work on.

Another common trait of an Aries moon is that you likely have competitive tendencies. You may get easily threatened by the success of others and you could feel the need to always be right or come out on top. Rather than pitting yourself against other people, though, you are better off channeling your energy into a hobby or sport that you truly love. As you can accumulate so much pent-up energy, you may want to have some sort of regular physical activity going on in your life. Exercising, traveling, or fully immersing yourself in your next big project will help dissipate feelings of impatience or frustration.

TAURUS MOON

If your moon is in Taurus, you like to approach life at your own pace. You may have little rituals and routines, and you want to maintain a sense of peace and groundedness within yourself that you can turn to when everything else feels chaotic. You may prefer first observing unfamiliar situations or people instead of jumping right in and sharing details about yourself. You need to feel secure within a relationship and build a sense of deep trust with someone before you feel comfortable expressing the full extent of your emotions.

If there is one thing you dislike, it is when people rush you or try telling you what to do. You can be very set in your ways, and if you sense that someone is trying to push you into something, you will respond by digging in your heels and refusing to change your mind. You might get criticized for moving too slowly, but it's just because you need to process how you're feeling before you confront an issue or make a big decision. A day-to-day example might be that, if you have decided to stay in and watch television on a Saturday night, it will be almost impossible for your friends to convince you to change plans and go out. Once your mind is made up, you are not easily swayed, and you can be quite stubborn, especially if you feel like your way is the best way. Learning how to be more flexible and open-minded to changes in plans, especially those proposed in your close relationships, is something that you may need to work on.

As a Taurus moon, you are also highly sensual and may crave a lot of physical touch in your relationships. You're very receptive to how things look, smell, and feel, and you appreciate romantic gestures, such as a candlelit dinner, a couples massage, or receiving thoughtful gifts. You might be drawn to romantic partners who dress well or have a shared appreciation for the finer things in life. Beyond the material, though, above all you seek consistency from the people you date. Trust is something that people have to earn from you, and if someone says they are going to show up, you will hold them to it. You have low tolerance for unpredictable behavior; when you commit to someone, you're in it for the long haul. You may also hold on to relationships for too long, though, being unable to end things even if it's not working out. From your perspective, it might be that you don't want to have put in all that effort for nothing. You can sometimes be quite possessive in romantic situations, so it's important that you recognize if the relationship is something that is truly serving you or if it's time to walk away.

Annabel says she often deals with the more complicated, controlling side of having a Taurus moon. "I've been cheated on in the past, so I need someone who does exactly what they say. I still have a great fear of being abandoned." She also mentioned that trust and consistency are the top traits that she looks for in a partner.

The best way to combat any of these negative tendencies and to feel more grounded is to engage in slow activities that give a sense of peace and calm, such as cooking, going for a walk, engaging in arts and crafts, or building things with your hands. If you feel like a dating situation is getting out of control or you start experiencing stress in a relationship, you will need to find a way to connect with your physical surroundings and engage in the beauty of everyday life.

GEMINI MOON

If you have a Gemini moon, you are curious about the world around you, and you may know a little bit about a variety of subjects. Your mind runs at a million miles a minute, which is definitely helpful when it comes to keeping up with random facts and information. You may also thrive in social situations, and you enjoy getting other people's perspectives and trading ideas and opinions. It is through connecting with people on an intellectual level and having these interactions that you are better able to understand yourself. However, you can also be very "in your own head" at times, and you may end up overthinking certain situations. It might be challenging for you to be alone and simply feel your emotions, because your first instinct is to analyze everything or discuss it with someone. By always trying to anticipate what's coming next or running through how you could have said something differently to someone, you end up worrying yourself for no reason. Additionally, you may get easily distracted and find it hard to focus on just one task at a time. Someone might be talking to you, or you may be watching television, and you will completely zone out with your thoughts, having wandered off to another topic entirely. Being fully present in your relationships is a skill you are learning how to master.

When dating, you are probably most attracted to people who are witty and intelligent. Communication is key for you, so you need a partner who has a good sense of humor, with whom you can enjoy a playful back and forth. You usually excel at first dates because you're skilled at small talk and helping others feel at ease. However, when it's time to go deeper, you may start to panic. Talking about profound emotions or what you want in a relationship may make you feel uncomfortable. At times, you might also be indecisive about whether or not you like someone, preferring to keep your options open for the fear of missing out.

Coco, who has a Gemini moon, says that she easily grows bored with people, especially during the getting-to-know-you stage. Though she likes to use dating apps, she says, ". . . usually I never even make it to the first date. There has to be banter and an intellectual connection first." She adds that it's often difficult to know what she's even feeling for someone. "I'm always in my head—I never feel my feelings, I just think about them. It can be hard to know what I'm looking for because I'm so all over the place."

Finding ways to calm your thoughts will help when you're feeling overwhelmed by dating, a relationship, or life in general. With your moon in Gemini, you will want to engage your mind in topics that light you up and take you out of your own head. You may enjoy regularly listening to podcasts, reading multiple books at once, journaling about your feelings, or taking workshops or courses on subjects that pique your interest.

CANCER MOON

If you have your moon in Cancer, you probably like to take care of people and are frequently supporting those closest to you. You might be a great listener, and people come to you with their problems knowing that you will give good advice and won't judge or criticize them. Though you're outgoing around the people you're comfortable with, you may come across as shy when first meeting someone. It may take time for you to feel fully comfortable opening up and sharing your personality. Even if you present as calm and reserved, you typically have pretty strong emotions going on beneath the surface. You can be pretty sensitive and take a lot of what you're told to heart or dwell excessively on the past. Your moods may fluctuate quite a bit, too, and, on any given day, you might go through a number of emotional highs and lows. You may be learning not to take every rude comment or criticism personally, in an understanding that other people's negativity is not your problem.

When dating, you may look for someone with whom you could start a home and family. You crave familiarity, so you may be most attracted to people who come from a similar background or who you already know. Putting yourself out there both socially and romantically may feel a bit scary, and casual dating could be tough for you to navigate because you crave deeper connections and a sense of security with the other person. You need authentic, emotional exchanges to feel satisfied. Additionally, you may have a strong bond to your family or the place you grew up, and there may be a desire to stay close to home. On the other hand, if your family relationships weren't the greatest, there may be some lingering element of your early home life that you have to work through in your adult relationships. Aside from family, your home tends to be your safe space, and you may choose staying in over going out and socializing for the majority of the time.

One area that you may struggle with is letting people know when you're upset. You could have a habit of holding onto past hurts and resentments, not easily forgetting anyone who has previously upset you. To avoid frustrations in a relationship building up over time, it is important to work on communicating openly with people and letting your partner know what's on your mind. As a Cancer moon, you will need to focus on nurturing yourself in the same ways you do for other people. You may want to carve out time each week for a self-care day, or you could enjoy comforting activities like cooking or having movie nights at home by yourself. Spending time with family or forming a network of friends that feels as close as family will also be good for your well-being. By creating a stable and comfortable home environment for yourself, you will be able to show up as a better partner in your relationships.

LEO MOON

If you have a Leo moon, you are a natural creative and may need some sort of artistic hobby or outlet for self-expression to feel emotionally fulfilled. You have a lot of enthusiasm for the things you care about. Additionally, you could have a very silly sense of humor and, even into old age, maintain an almost childlike spirit where you never take yourself too seriously. All of these traits make you good with children—you may particularly enjoy the experience of parenting, or working with children could somehow play into your career. Even if that's not the case, you will still enjoy getting into a creative flow and being able to pour your full personality into an aspect of your work. You may have a deep desire to feel recognized and appreciated by others, and you could want to create something that stands the test of time.

However, you can also get a bit dramatic if you feel like you are not being listened to. Little disagreements may get blown out of proportion and you can get very heated, especially if you feel disrespected. You tend to be hyperaware of how other people see you and feel as if every little flaw or word that comes out wrong is there for the world to see. In a way, you may view your life as one big performance, with you as the main character. You can also be quite sensitive and may need frequent positive feedback to feel good about yourself. You could try to cover up your insecurities by always being the funny one in the friendship group or even poking fun at yourself.

This need for attention may be heightened in your dating life. When you decide you like someone, you could zero in on that person, becoming jealous if you sense that they are talking to other people. A deep fear of rejection may make it hard for you to be vulnerable when dating. You may also have a habit of fishing for compliments with your significant other and needing constant reassurance that the relationship is okay.

Dan, who has his moon in Leo, describes his approach to dating. "All the men I go after are people I think are objectively hot, and I feel validated when I'm able to conquer them." He says that he gets frustrated when someone doesn't seem to be interested in him. He takes their indifference to heart, viewing it as indicating that he's not attractive enough for them. "I think it's really scary to be vulnerable and open up and know that the relationship might end. When I do find someone who checks my boxes, I get scared. Rejection is extremely scary."

Instead of trying so hard to people-please, your biggest challenge as a Leo moon is learning how to build self-confidence all on your own. You can't always rely on external sources to tell you that you're doing a good job or that you're attractive enough. The best way to gain greater self-esteem is in finding some type of creative outlet or a passion outside of work that you can pour your energy into. By prioritizing the activities that light you up, you won't be so quick to toss your needs aside to please a potential partner.

VIRGO MOON

If your moon is in Virgo, you like to feel productive and of service to other people. You're probably extremely attentive to detail, never forgetting a partner or friend's birthday or any other important life events. You're always putting a lot of thought into what you think will make another person happy. As for yourself, you may constantly be thinking up ways you can improve upon certain aspects of your life, such as eliminating negative habits or finding ways to better streamline your schedule, eat healthier, or exercise more regularly. You hold yourself and your romantic partners to high standards, but you have to be mindful of sometimes being too critical of others.

When dating, a relationship has to make sense in your life at that particular moment in order for you to even entertain the idea. You might be very particular about who you decide to date, with a list of traits you're looking for in a partner. I have a close friend who is a Virgo moon, and she keeps a spreadsheet of dates she's been on. Her belief is that the more people she goes out with, the more likely it is that she will meet her future partner. As a Pisces moon myself, I am a hopeless romantic and have a hard time wrapping my head around her analytical approach to finding love.

As a Virgo moon, your biggest challenge to overcome is learning that it's okay not to be perfect all of the time. You may strive hard to be the best partner or come across in a certain light, but in worrying so much about small, relatively insignificant details, you could end up stressing yourself for no reason and losing out on being present in the relationship. Little mistakes you make aren't the reason someone ghosts you or a relationship ultimately doesn't work out. It is not worth beating yourself up over everything you may have done wrong. In addition, when you're feeling nervous or upset, you might have the tendency to nag at your partner's imperfections instead of looking at the real root cause of your feelings. Though you mean well, and you're just trying to help and make someone's life easier, constant criticism will only end up pushing your partner further away.

At times, you may find yourself with an overabundance of nervous energy, finding it difficult to relax and do nothing. You may feel like you always need to stay productive, be accomplishing something or improving upon some aspect of your life. The best way to channel any pent-up energy is to develop a regular, daily routine that helps soothe both your mind and body. You may find solace in practicing wellness activities such as yoga or meditation, and you will feel noticeably more at peace when you're taking care of your body and incorporating physical movement into your daily life. You could also seek a job or side activity that involves giving back to others.

LIBRA MOON

If you have your moon in Libra, you like to foster close one-on-one connections with people, and you may choose catching up with a good friend or staying in with a romantic partner over attending a huge social outing any day. You may even feel more comfortable when you are partnered up, and you end up establishing a greater sense of identity for yourself through your relationships. For instance, if you're making a huge life change, you may first want to seek feedback from someone close to you. You like to be able to weigh your ideas against those of another person because it helps you to see what you want more clearly. Within a romantic relationship, your partner may be able to point out different strengths you have or talents that you should tap into. Additionally, you may thrive in a career that has a heavy emphasis on client relationships or where you're talking to people regularly in intimate settings.

Establishing balance in your relationships is very important to you. You're often taking note of whether the other person is putting in as much effort as you are, and you might be quick to see when things are unequal. You want to see everyone treated fairly, and you may speak out when you notice that the balance is off, either in your own relationships or in society at large. You also have a natural eye for beauty, and you tend to know what looks good. You probably have a particular aesthetic when it comes to clothing, art, travel, and interior design, and you may be drawn to people who are just as cultured. In addition, you place great value on having good manners. There is no bigger turn-off than a person who is rude, loud in public, or not socially adept. Presenting well and carrying oneself with elegance are traits that you might seek in a partner.

You may, however, have a tendency to get too caught up in wondering what everyone else thinks, instead of being confident in voicing your own personal opinions. As a Libra moon, your biggest challenge is overcoming your fear of conflict. You may have a reputation for never making up your mind because you don't want your decisions to cause anyone to feel annoyed or upset with you. These qualities may make it hard for you to stand up for yourself when dating, and you could end up putting up with more than you should from people. You may have a pattern of ending up with someone who acts as the direct and assertive partner in the relationship, and their needs could end up overshadowing your own. Once you learn how to prioritize your desires and speak up about how you're feeling, you won't attract people who are so demanding.

You're quick to prioritize your relationships, so it's necessary for you to step back from time to time and make sure that you're achieving balance in all areas of your life. You don't want to lose yourself when you're around other people, and you may feel most fulfilled when digging deeper into hobbies and interests that involve communication, such as writing, podcasting, or projects related to design and creativity. Additionally, you could feel at peace when traveling or teaching yourself new knowledge about the world around you.

SCORPIO MOON

If your moon is in Scorpio, you probably like your privacy and may not be so open about your emotions. Though your feelings can be all-consuming and intense, you tend to keep them buried and you like to remain in control over how much of yourself you reveal to other people. When dating, you crave deep connections with people from the start. You prefer to skip the small talk, as you would much rather get to the bottom of who someone really is. You may have a natural interest in learning about psychology, human behavior, and what makes people tick, and these passions may even play into your career somehow. In addition, you're skilled at remaining strong in the face of crisis and are naturally calm, cool, and collected when you are helping people through their problems.

In your love life, you might be very selective about who you decide to date, and you're immediately able to sense if someone is worth knowing. You're either not interested in someone at all or completely obsessed with one particular person. However, you don't usually let on how much you like someone and may spend months harboring a crush or observing the other person from afar. You may not seem to have as many relationships or flings as your friends, since you like holding out for someone special. If you don't feel passionately about a person, you don't often see any point in pursuing them further.

Along with her Scorpio moon, Ava also has her sun, Mercury, and Venus in Scorpio. She is extremely selective about who she dates or hooks up with and admits that the people she does have feelings for are usually male friends rather than total strangers. "I'm looking for a high-quality relationship and won't settle for anything else. I need someone who I can connect with emotionally and intellectually, which is hard to find in general, and especially hard to find at my age." She adds that she's holding out for a relationship that is lasting and transformative, rather than jumping into something that is fleeting and casual. Even if it's not forever, she wants a relationship that she will remember for the rest of her life.

If you have a Scorpio moon, a big lesson that you may repeatedly face is around learning that you aren't always in control. You may often have suspicions that the other person you like will end up leaving you, or you may be quick to break off situationships first to avoid getting your heart broken or being seen as weak or vulnerable. With the people that you do date, you may struggle with jealousy or controlling tendencies. Developing greater trust in your partner and having faith that a relationship will turn out as it should might be areas that you need to work on.

Relationships are often a point of transformation for you, and you may walk away from any romantic situation, no matter how short or long it was, with a feeling that you've learned something significant about yourself. When you find yourself falling into the trap of obsessive thinking about what could happen in a relationship, try to channel this intensity into areas that you can actually control, such as your career, a passion project, or doing inner healing work on yourself. By turning your focus back to the things that make you excited, you will experience less frustration in your relationships.

SAGITTARIUS MOON

If you have your moon in Sagittarius, you have a love of knowledge and adventure. You might be a big fan of traveling and are always looking to learn more about the world around you, whether by going back to school for another degree in an inspiring subject, doing self-motivated research, or immersing yourself in a foreign culture to gain a different perspective on life. You may also have a natural ability as a teacher, getting other people excited about the same topics that light you up. You need a lot of freedom and space within your daily life. You like being able to act on a whim without feeling held back in any way. Settling into a solid routine and focusing on the mundane details of everyday life may pose a challenge for you, as you prefer to think in terms of the bigger picture. You might spend a lot of time reflecting on the meaning of life or why you are the way you are. You could feel very connected to a set of spiritual beliefs and find yourself attracted to people who push you to think differently. Intelligence is a big turn-on for you.

In your relationships, you like to try out new experiences and feel like you're constantly growing with your partner. You appreciate someone who will challenge you and push you out of your comfort zone, but you could get easily bored if it feels like the other person isn't as open-minded or curious as you. You may also surround yourself with people from different cultural backgrounds or who have lived abroad extensively because you find them interesting to be around. It could take you some time to fully commit to someone, as you don't want to feel like your freedom is being restricted. You might get worried that you're missing out on fun new experiences by being in a relationship.

Maya, who has a Sagittarius moon, describes her ideal partner as "someone who is okay with going deep, and who can self-reflect. They don't necessarily need to be a world traveler or from another culture, but I value the mentality of always wanting to learn and expand. I also don't think I could be with someone long term who doesn't read a lot."

As a Sagittarius moon, your first response to any type of difficult situation may be to find the lesson in it. Obstacles don't usually deter you, and you view every challenge as a necessary growth experience. Though you're good at remaining upbeat and positive, this can sometimes be frustrating for your partner or the people closest to you. You may go out of your way to avoid discussing difficult topics, not understanding that it's actually okay to address areas of distress or encounter conflict with people. Sometimes, relationships do call for you to be serious.

Because you're prone to feeling restless when a relationship falls into a steady routine, you may need to develop some sort of outlet where you can go off and do your own thing from time to time. If you're unable to travel, you may find enjoyment in reading, writing, teaching people, or leaning into your spirituality. Focusing on any of these areas will help you to feel more emotionally fulfilled and at peace.

CAPRICORN MOON

If you have your moon in Capricorn, you might have always felt like the mature or responsible one growing up, and you may have had to take on a lot of responsibility from a young age. As an adult, it's possible you now put a lot of pressure on yourself to succeed and have a desire to be recognized for your achievements. Your career is likely a big priority for you, and you may work really hard to accomplish specific goals at work or be seen as an expert in a specific field. You're also pretty self-reliant, so when it comes to relationships it could take you a while to open up and show your softer side. It may feel a bit scary to rely on someone else or even accept another person taking care of you. You're probably guarded with your emotions, wishing to avoid coming across as needy. It definitely takes a while for you to let your guard down and show that you have feelings for someone.

Natalia, who has her moon in Capricorn, shares what she has struggled with the most when dating: "I have to constantly remind myself that guys like people who like them. Sometimes I have to force myself to show them that I am interested and give them affection." She admits that men tell her she gives off "friend vibes," because she finds it so difficult to show how she feels.

You might be wary of people at first when dating, not taking a serious interest in someone until they have proven themselves to be a capable partner. Whether in friendship or romance, you don't commit to just anyone. You're probably drawn to people who are ambitious and have their life together and may only entertain a relationship if you feel like it has long-term potential. One other thing to note, if you have a Capricorn moon, is that you will probably gain a greater understanding over your emotional self as you get older, specifically around the time you transition from your late twenties into your thirties. Before then, your personal life may not be the main focus, and it could feel like everyone else is ahead of you in their relationships. Because you take relationship commitment so seriously, it might be difficult for you to engage in casual flings or online dating in the same way that your friends do. As you get older, it can be refreshing to find that other people your age finally want to settle down, too.

Because you're so busy chasing your goals, you often avoid sitting with any uncomfortable emotions or find it hard to just relax and have fun. You can be very critical of yourself and the people you date. You should try to schedule periodic downtime or find hobbies outside of your job that you enjoy doing. Try working on projects just for you, not because it is what is expected of you or what you think will please other people. When you get clear on what makes you truly happy, rather than simply chasing external validation and achievements, you won't be as likely to vent as much criticism or take your frustration out on the people you date.

AQUARIUS MOON

If your moon is in Aquarius, you have probably always felt different from everyone else. No matter how many people you surround yourself with, it could still seem like you're an outsider looking in. Not fitting in isn't a bad thing at all; rather, it is what pushes you to be so unique and innovative. You're not someone who conforms to group mentality, and you like to maintain your independence. You are also able to envision an ideal future for society, and you may enjoy backing causes that you care about or being a part of a community that promotes change in the world. Because you are so often thinking about what's next, though, you may get too caught up in the future, finding it difficult to stay grounded in the present moment.

When it comes to dating, you march to the beat of your own drum. You might be drawn to people who are different—the quirkier the better. You may rebel against traditional relationship rules as well, preferring to experiment with having an open relationship or enjoying long-distance partnerships. Your sexuality may also be more fluid, or you don't let someone's gender determine whether or not you're attracted to them. With dating, you may actively veer away from what is expected of you, ignoring the idea that you need to be married by a particular age or must wait a certain number of dates to sleep with someone.

The biggest challenge you could face in relationships, though, is that you can be very "in your own head," causing other people to see you as aloof or uninterested. It may be difficult for you to fully relax with someone new, or you could find it uncomfortable sharing your emotions and being outwardly affectionate with people. You may also have a real fear of losing your identity in relationships, getting spooked if you sense the person you're seeing is too clingy or expects too much commitment early on. Being a bit detached does have its benefits: instead of instantly reacting when you're facing conflict with your partner, you are able to momentarily pause and reflect on what your next response should be.

Martha, an Aquarius moon, describes the difficulty she's had tapping into her emotional self. "Throughout my early twenties I leaned into acting uninterested when dating, because I thought it was the cool thing to do. I had to actively use therapy to work out how to access my emotions. It used to be that I couldn't even talk about my feelings."

As an Aquarius moon, it is necessary to get out of your head and learn how to better prioritize your physical health. You may feel like it's hard to shut off the constant stream of commentary that is running through your mind, so finding ways to connect with your body will help you feel more grounded. Developing a regular meditation practice, going on daily walks, or finding ways to add regular exercise into your schedule will help you immensely, so that you leave any nervous energy at the door and stay present in your relationships.

PISCES MOON

With a Pisces moon, your first instinct is to nurture and help others through their problems. You are very intuitive and can easily empathize with people, offering helpful advice and compassion. You tend to know exactly what other people need to hear, and you may get strong gut feelings or an inner sense about certain situations. At times, though, it may be difficult to decipher what emotions are yours and what energy you may have picked up from someone else. You are acutely sensitive to the world around you, so having space to be alone is necessary in order to reflect on your feelings and recharge your batteries.

When it comes to your love life, you might be a bit obsessed with romance. Pisces is a sign that likes to transcend reality, so you will want to feel like you're having a soul-bonding experience with someone that goes way beyond the surface level. However, you may often approach relationships with rose-tinted glasses, seeing only the potential of who this other person could be and ignoring any red flags that are right in front of you. Your natural tendency is to be giving toward others, but you could get trapped into trying to fix the people you date. You may pour all of your energy into making it work with someone, going out of your way to do little favors for them. Along the way, though, you may end up forgetting your own hobbies and interests.

Your emotions might sometimes feel overwhelming, and you could fall prey to escapist tendencies like becoming isolated, losing yourself in the people you date, partying a lot, or binge-watching TV. Rather than running away from your feelings or looking for a romantic partner to give you a sense of self, it can be helpful to find something bigger than yourself to connect to in your everyday life. For example, you may want to get in touch with your inner world through practicing meditation, yoga, or even astrology. Having some sort of creative pursuit, community service activity, or simply allowing yourself the space to daydream would be good, too. There is a need to direct some of your empathetic, nurturing energy toward taking care of yourself rather than always trying to save other people.

As a Pisces moon myself, whenever I would date someone, even if it was nothing serious, the other person's interests would automatically become my interests. I would forget that I had a life outside of that person, so, when we broke up, it would hit me all the harder because I had forgotten who I was. I would build up these elaborate fantasies of how I was going to get married to some guy I had been on two dates with, and I would be crushed when reality failed to match my expectations. I wanted instant intimacy with someone, but as I got older, I learned that it takes time to build relationships—I couldn't expect to know everything about someone immediately. Through finding astrology and meditation and exploring other realms of spirituality, I was able to find peace with my inner self, rather than trying to cling on to any guy that so much as looked at me.

CHAPTER 6

How You Relate to Others: Venus and Mars

We now have a firm grasp on your moon sign and how it may manifest in your personality, so let's move on to Venus and Mars. Whereas the moon speaks to the ways in which you feel nourished and most at home in a relationship, Venus and Mars show your style of relating to others as well as what traits you find attractive in another person. Before we jump into these two planets through the various signs, let's examine Venus and Mars a little more closely to fully understand why they are so important when it comes to love.

Venus represents:
- Your likes and dislikes, as well as what you find attractive
- Your personal taste and aesthetic
- How you give and receive affection
- Your values
- How you like to spend money
- Your style of relating to other people

Venus is the planet that embodies your personal taste, so its placement in your birth chart will indicate what initially draws you to someone, what you desire in a partner, and how you go about getting to know that person. Do you jump into relationships really quickly with a lot of passion, or are you someone who takes dating at a slower pace, preferring to first weigh all of your options? You can also think of Venus as your love language, as it shows how you like to give and receive affection. In addition to romantic relationships, Venus reveals how you maintain friendships and how much you rely on other people in general.

Venus is key to understanding your interests and what you deem to be beautiful. The sign it is placed in can reveal what type of hobbies you like to pursue, the music you enjoy listening to, and your aesthetic when it comes to clothing or interior design. It also represents your approach to finances and what items you consider worth spending your money on. All of these elements are important to know when dating, because ideally you will want a partner who is similarly aligned with your values.

Mars represents:

- How you act on your desires
- How you approach conflict
- What turns you on and your sexual desires
- What motivates you
- Your energy levels and how you like to work

By contrast, Mars indicates how you go after what you want and how you act on your desires. Even outside of relationships, it is a planet that reveals what motivates you and what activities you enjoy putting your energy and effort toward. Its sign placement can show whether you're comfortable making the first move when dating or if you would rather be pursued by a potential partner. Mars also has more to do with the act of sex than Venus does. It indicates what turns you on, how much or how little you may like to have sex, and how much weight you place on the physical aspect of the relationship. For example, if Mars is in a water sign like Pisces, the person may need a strong emotional bond to whomever they're sleeping with. One-night stands or casual hook-ups are probably not something they can do easily. If Mars is in an air sign like Gemini, the person may crave more of a mental connection with another person, and it's the ability to have interesting conversations with the person they're dating that turns them on. Additionally, Mars shows how you approach conflict within your relationships, so it can reveal if you're direct and upfront about what's bothering you or if you tend to act passively, keeping frustrations to yourself. Understanding this aspect of your Mars sign is important because you may want to improve upon how you address problems with your partner or work on being more open about why you're upset.

When it comes to the placement of both these planets in the chart, you may notice that you end up attracting partners who embody the traits of your Venus and Mars signs, rather than fully embracing them yourself. Your romantic interests may mirror back to you the qualities that you feel you are missing. From personal experience with my Mars in Cancer, I am embarrassed to admit that I usually look to my partner to take care of me, cook for me, and nurture me, instead of fulfilling these needs on my own. Only recently have I started to put energy into these Cancerian-type activities. Another example may be a person who has their Venus in Aries. They might be drawn to partners who are direct, confident, and take initiative, especially if they feel like they are lacking in these qualities. Try to keep this tidbit of information in mind when reading both your Venus and Mars signs.

As we get into this chapter, you may also encounter some contradictions with your sign placements. Not everyone is going to have their moon, Venus, and Mars in the same sign or even the same element, and that is what makes us complex human beings. You may have your moon in an adventure-seeking, risk-taking sign like Sagittarius, while your Mars is in a very practical, grounded sign like Capricorn, which you might resonate with a bit more. Try to remember that it takes time—often your entire lifetime—to fully grow into and embrace all parts of your birth chart, so don't get caught up in thinking that one planet is more important to you than another.

Take the time now to locate the signs of both Venus and Mars in your birth chart and read the passages relevant to your placements below. If one or both of these planets happen to be in the same sign as your moon, there might be some repetition, but hopefully you can still see how the planets function a bit differently.

ARIES VENUS AND MARS

Aries is a sign that is direct about what it wants. If you have your Venus or Mars in this fire sign, you may get really hyped up and excited about new love interests. You typically aren't shy about your feelings, and when you encounter someone that you do like you are eager to have it develop into something romantic immediately. You don't have much patience for waiting around and seeing if the other person is going to make a move. The people you are naturally drawn to probably share your same passionate energy, and you like having a partner who is spontaneous and willing to try out new experiences. Rather than suggesting your typical "let's grab drinks," you prefer when your dates suggest an activity or experience. Aside from when you're first getting to know someone, it's also crucial that you find ways to keep the excitement alive with a long-term partner, because you may grow restless with the same old routine day-in and day-out.

"I used to fall in love all the time when I was younger," shares Nora, who has her Venus in Aries. "I would just meet someone and immediately like their vibe." Nora finds, though, that if someone doesn't reciprocate those same feelings she moves on just as quickly. "My emotions are all-encompassing at first, and all I can think about is this one person. But then something will inevitably happen, and I'm just over it."

This ability to walk away without appearing to be too hurt is typical of Aries. With either Venus or Mars in this sign, you may take pride in how independent you are, but you could also have a fear of coming across as needy. It might be difficult for you to admit when you need help from your partner or friends, as you may see this as a sign of weakness. Being someone who is so self-sufficient, you may have a hard time empathizing with people who aren't the same. You are used to putting your own needs first, but in your relationships, you will need to be mindful of taking the other person into consideration and being sensitive to what they want.

Venus in Aries thrives on being out and about in the world, coming into contact with people. You're quite friendly, and even if you've been hurt in the past, you still approach new relationships with a lot of enthusiasm. Your dating life may usually be pretty active, and you aren't afraid to put yourself out there. Additionally, your ideal partner is probably someone who has their own life and is just as independent and action-oriented as you. You need to feel like you're constantly growing and learning within the relationship to keep things exciting, and you may want someone who shares that optimistic, can-do attitude. The way you go about relationships might be a bit impulsive, though, and you could be prone to jumping into things before considering whether you even like the other person. You can be quite competitive in all areas of your life, so it comes as no surprise that this behavior may carry over into your relationships. You may have a fear of other people getting ahead of you in love, and there might be an inner need to keep up. My dad, who has been married three times, has his Venus in Aries. After his first two marriages ended abruptly, he jokes about someone saying to him, "You know, you can just date people. You don't have to always marry them."

In addition to embodying many of the above traits, Mars in Aries is also good at making quick decisions and acting immediately. If you have this placement, you may be pretty comfortable with pinpointing your desires and being direct about how you're going to get there. You're rarely passive aggressive and will want to confront any relationship issues as soon as they arise. You may get angry fast but find your anger passes just as quickly, and you definitely don't hold onto grudges. In your relationships, you appreciate people who, like you, are blunt and to the point. You are a passionate person and, as such, the physical aspect of a relationship is very important to you—you might use sex as an outlet for all of your pent-up energy. You're also excited by newness, so you could have a lot of lust early on in a relationship. Your biggest challenge is in figuring out how to sustain those strong feelings over time. It could be smart to slow down when dating and figure out if someone is actually the right fit or if it's just the chase that you enjoy.

TAURUS VENUS AND MARS

Taurus loves comfort and stability in relationships. Those who have their Venus or Mars in this sign enjoy the physical closeness and security that comes from being committed to another person. You may still take it slow when you're first getting to know someone; you like to move at your own pace, which other people may sometimes call lazy, but you hate the feeling of being rushed into anything too soon. You can be very picky about who you like, which is certainly not a bad thing, and you may be drawn to people who dress well, have an eye for beauty, or who have the potential to financially provide for you. Before you get in too deep, you want to know that the other person adds value to your life and that the relationship has the potential to go the distance. You don't want to put all of your time and energy into someone for the relationship not to last.

However, your stubborn determination to make it work may sometimes lead you to stay in romantic relationships or friendships that have passed their expiration date. Accepting when it's time to relinquish control and move on may be a lesson that frequently pops up in your love life. Oftentimes, that need to be in control comes from feeling like your security in the relationship is threatened. When you feel uncertain about where you stand with someone or you're simply lacking confidence in yourself, you may end up behaving in an extra possessive way toward your partner.

With Venus in Taurus specifically, you have a naturally creative side, and you may like to spend your free time immersed in artistic hobbies. You have a deep love of beauty, and you may put a lot of effort into making your surroundings relaxing and aesthetically pleasing. You also aren't afraid to spend money and probably enjoy splurging on clothing, decorative homeware, or high-quality food. Your expensive taste and appreciation for the little pleasures in life carries over into your relationships as well. Ideally, you will want a partner who knows how to dress themselves well and treats you to nice dinners out or little gifts from time to time.

Because Taurus is the sign that is ruled by Venus, having your Venus fall in its "home" sign means that being part of a relationship is something that comes naturally to you, and you enjoy the comfortable routine that you fall into with another person. In addition, you may crave a lot of physical affection and touch. "I'll sometimes follow my boyfriend around the house because I like to be close to him. I'm always touching him and feeling his chest. It's very romantic and sensual to me to do that. Even if it's not in a sexual way, it just helps me to feel closer to him," Olivia, who has Venus in Taurus, shares.

Everything mentioned above may also apply if you have your Mars in Taurus. What sets this placement apart, though, is its slow, steady approach to dating. These tendencies clash with the inherent qualities of Mars, a planet associated with acting immediately and often impulsively. If you have Mars in Taurus, you will therefore be very persistent when you want something, and in relationships you will have the patience to either pursue someone over an extended period of time or wait until the other person approaches you. In the bedroom you can be quite sensual; physical touch is reassuring for you and allows you to feel much more emotionally close to someone.

Outside of dating, you have to be passionate about whatever you're working toward, or you may not see the point in exerting your energy at all. You don't appreciate when people try to push you into making a decision or pressure you to agree with them—this will only make you dig your heels in further and stick to your own path.

However, you're not one to get visibly angry, and it might be difficult for other people to tell when you're upset. You like to maintain a sense of control in all areas of your life, so additionally you may require independence within your job or space outside of work to engage in calming pastimes like cooking, going for walks in nature, enjoying the arts, or doing any type of hands-on activity.

GEMINI VENUS AND MARS

Gemini is endlessly curious: it is the zodiac sign that usually knows a little bit about a million different topics. If you have your Venus or Mars in Gemini, you probably find enjoyment in communication-based pursuits like reading, writing, doing word puzzles, or learning new skills quickly on the spot. It may even be challenging for you to sit still, as your mind is usually one step ahead of you, figuring out what subject it wants to embark on next. Your encyclopedic knowledge definitely comes in handy on first dates and in social situations, as you are able to make small talk with just about anyone. In fact, you may thrive in environments where you can connect with lots of different people, trading ideas and sharing what you know. You probably have a wide network of friends who you like to keep in frequent contact with by having quick calls or an ongoing group chat.

In terms of a romantic partner, you need someone who can go with the flow and keep up with your busy lifestyle. One of your natural talents is your eloquence, so your date must be able to engage in playful banter with you. You may love the initial stages of talking to someone because you genuinely enjoy flirting and crafting texts. Lucas, who has both his Venus and Mars in Gemini, describes how he is often attracted to someone's mind before their physical appearance. "Before I get sexual with someone, I go through a process of mental evaluation. Can we have a conversation for hours upon hours about anything and everything? I always suss that out on the first and second dates and use that as my barometer of whether or not I'm going to take things further and actually pursue the relationship."

With either of these Gemini placements, it may take a while for you to settle down and commit. The other person has to be interesting and multifaceted enough to hold your attention, and if that curiosity to get to know all their different sides isn't there, you could easily grow bored. Another challenge you may face with dating is your tendency to overthink. When you like someone, you may run through scenarios of why they fit into your life and how the relationship would make sense, rather than connecting with your feelings for them or figuring out if they are actually a good partner for you. You could also be a bit wishy-washy in your emotions toward people—you might be into someone one week but over it the next.

For those of you with Venus in Gemini specifically, you probably come across as cheerful and friendly. It's easy for you to make new friends and mingle. You like to regularly switch up who you hang out with as well, and you need variety when dating. You don't want to go to the same old restaurants and bars; you would much rather the other person suggest a different type of experience. Outside of relationships, you have a way with words, as well as the ability to synthesize a lot of information and get your ideas across in a way that other people can easily understand. You're probably drawn to partners who are equally as intelligent and can hold their own in a conversation. You may frequently change your mind about who you like, though, and you need a lot of space when seeing someone to reflect on your feelings and carefully consider what a relationship with that person would look like. There's nothing worse than someone coming on too strong or putting pressure on you to commit.

If you have Mars in Gemini, you may have quite a bit of anxious energy, and you could feel like you need to be occupying your mind at all times. On the other hand, you may not know exactly where to concentrate your efforts, because you have so many different interests that you would like to pursue. You may often feel pulled in multiple directions and that you're a jack of all trades, but a master of none. Some of this energy may carry over into your relationships, and you could get worried about making the right decision with a romantic interest. Your heart and your head may often be at odds, making you indecisive about which one to act on. Because you can get so caught up in your own thoughts, it may also be hard to fully enjoy physical intimacy with a partner. Finding ways to feel more grounded and connected to your body is important, and this may start by simply establishing concrete daily routines and rituals.

CANCER VENUS AND MARS

Cancer is the sign associated with the home, so if your Venus or Mars is found in this sign, your main priority when dating might be to find a partner with whom you can settle down and build a solid home and family life together. There's also the desire to nurture whomever you're dating, making sure that they always feel comfortable and taken care of. On the flip side of that, though, you may end up attracting people who you know will do all of the above for you. You could seek out a partner who loves to cook, clean, or who has the potential to be a good parent. In both friendships and romantic relationships, no matter what your gender is, you may take on the role of the maternal figure, whom other people turn to for help. You're easily able to empathize with others, and you have a soft way of delivering advice. However, you may want to be wary of always placing the other person's needs above your own or losing a part of your identity when you're in a relationship.

"I always pick people I can take care of and nurture," says Kathy, who has her Venus in Cancer. Recalling the beginning of the relationship with her now husband, she says, "The first time we ever hung out, I was like: 'Come over to my house. I've made you homemade lasagne, I've made bread, I've made dessert. And let's just hang out and watch a movie.'"

You may have a traditional approach to dating and could be fond of upholding certain rules and expectations. You like to be pursued and asked on dates and will want to go through those necessary steps to get to know the other person. You're probably shy at first when you like someone, not readily expressing your emotions, and you might be extra sensitive to rejection. Even though you crave emotional closeness with a person, it can feel scary putting yourself out there and making a move. You need to feel safe and like you can fully trust the other person before letting your guard down. Though you may not make it obvious, you develop strong attachments to people quickly.

For those of you who have Venus in Cancer, you might be especially into interior design, adding little touches to make your space feel comfortable and cozy. There is a need for a safe place you can return to at the end of the day. You might also hold onto items that have either been passed down through generations or hold a lot of sentimental value to you or be fond of antiques and vintage clothing. You are good at maintaining relationships and may still be friends with people you've known since childhood, with friends who feel like an extension of your family. You may be a bit shy when thrown into unfamiliar social situations, and it definitely takes you a while to warm up to new people. Romantically, you are attracted to partners that place that same emphasis and importance on home life and need someone who recognizes your need for privacy and space.

If you have your Mars in Cancer, you may have strong emotional reactions—you could have a tendency to either react quickly in the heat of the moment, or let your feelings simmer beneath the surface. When you're angry, you could also end up simultaneously teary-eyed and emotional. You may talk about how frustrated you are, but, when it comes down to confronting someone, you may shy away from being direct and addressing the issue at hand. However, you will never ever forget anyone who has ever wronged you, and it may take you a long time to get over grudges or relationships that ended badly. You may also have the desire to fiercely protect your friends, family, and home, and you may get worked up over anyone who doesn't respect your living space. Doing things for other people comes naturally to you, but it may be more difficult to nurture yourself in the same way or pinpoint what you really want to put your energy toward. The work you do needs to hold a deeper meaning in order for you to feel excited and motivated by it. If your heart isn't in it, you will get burned out easily. As for the physical aspect of relationships, you are fond of cuddling, being close to the other person, and feeling needed by them. Sometimes, having this type of intimacy can be more important than the actual act of sex.

LEO VENUS AND MARS

Leo has a flair for the dramatic. If you have your Venus or Mars in this sign, you may wear your heart on your sleeve, with a childlike playfulness and silly sense of humor that other people find fun to be around. You also like having attention on you and want to be fawned over by the people you date. You enjoy when the person you're seeing goes out of their way to plan romantic gestures for you, like surprising you with flowers or arranging a candlelit dinner. However, you may experience a lot of ups and downs in your love life. You can go from zero to a hundred very quickly, and you're either not interested in someone at all or feel extremely passionately about the relationship. You're fiercely loyal to both your friends and romantic partners and may like to talk people up with compliments and praise. However, the second someone betrays your trust or disrespects you, you are done. Relationships do not always end on friendly terms where you're concerned, and the biggest conflicts may often stem from feeling underappreciated or not respected by your partner. To avoid having such emotional highs and lows, you may want to be a bit more discerning from the start as to who you choose to open up to.

"When I'm interested in someone, I want their full, unwavering attention," says Charlotte, who has her Venus in Leo. She describes how her feelings for people are strong right from the start: "I've never been on a sixth date and still wondering where things are going. I meet someone, and I immediately hate them or immediately really like them." Having either your Venus or Mars in Leo definitely brings an intensity to your love life.

Outside of relationships, you thrive in creative environments, so you may have a career that allows you to put forth your full personality and artistic skills. As an example, actors, artists, stylists, or designers will often have either their Venus or Mars in Leo. You might also be drawn to people who work in a similar industry or who simply have a lot of passion for whatever they do. Additionally, appearance is of the utmost importance to you; you're very aware of how people see you, and you put careful consideration into how you dress and present yourself. When you're in a relationship, you want both you and your partner to look good when you walk into a room. Because you can get so hyper-focused on how you are perceived by others, you may obsess too much over minor details or mishaps.

Venus in Leo is known for its great sense of style and personal aesthetic. You come across as warm and affectionate, but typically only with people you know really well. If you're only in the early stages of dating, you might be pretty shy to reach out and text first for fear of being rejected. You also crave attention from your partner and want to feel seen and listened to by the other person. You may need frequent reassurances to feel secure in a relationship, and you could get easily jealous if you sense that the person you're dating is talking to other people—even if there hasn't yet been a conversation about exclusivity. Additionally, your self-worth may be very tied up in whether someone likes you or not, and you could desperately seek validation from romantic interests, making it hard to put aside the dating apps and just be alone. Ironically, though, it's when you spend time by yourself leaning into your solo activities that you are able to build greater confidence and self-esteem.

In addition to the above, Mars in Leo is very upfront and honest with people. If someone is bothering you, you're going to let them know exactly what is on your mind. However, you may sometimes be a little too blunt or blow things out of proportion, turning a small disagreement into a much bigger deal. You may bring a lot of drama into your relationships without even realizing it, so you need to make sure that you're being sensitive to other people's feelings rather than centering a problem entirely around yourself. These same theatrics are what make you so entertaining to be around, though, and people may light up in your presence because you're able to get them excited about new experiences or their future potential. You also take your own passion projects very seriously, and your work is often an extension of your identity. In addition to your career and the help you give to others, you put your whole heart into your relationships, and tend to be very demonstrative of your feelings for people.

VIRGO VENUS AND MARS

Virgo loves to be of service and is at its best when working hard and being productive. If you have your Venus or Mars in Virgo, you may be a very doting partner. You like doing small tasks that make someone's day easier and will go out of your way to put that extra effort into your relationships. You're also very attentive to the smallest details and you may make it a point to remember the information your partner has told you, whether that be an upcoming promotion at work or the name of their childhood dog. Additionally, you're focused on self-improvement, and you may enjoy taking care of your physical body through regular exercise, healthy eating, or having an elaborate skincare routine. It's critical that you have your alone time to engage in these routines and rituals to keep any anxiety or nervous energy at bay.

Virgo is ruled by Mercury, the planet associated with thoughts and communication, so you may be very "in your own head" and you could end up overthinking when it comes to dating, worrying about things like the wording of a text or feeling like you haven't done enough for your partner. You could have this inner need for everything to be perfect within your relationships, so you may go out of your way to accommodate the other person or try to fix all of their problems. Mackenzie, who has her Mars in Virgo, describes her need for close interactions to follow a certain order: "I'm very attuned to vibe shifts and energy changes. So, if I think that someone has said something that feels a bit off, I'm very receptive to that, and I ask, 'What's wrong? What did I do? Are you okay?' I automatically try to fix the situation to get everyone back to feeling positive."

After consistently giving to the people you date, you may come to realize that you have forgotten your own wants and needs in the process. Another way in which your perfectionist tendencies may come out is by being overly critical of other people. You hold yourself to high standards and could put a lot of pressure on yourself to succeed. However, you might end up fixating on other people's flaws just as much as your own, taking it upon yourself to improve your partner's life. To avoid constantly nagging or taking on a parent-like role in your relationships, you need to realize that it is not your duty to change someone. Rather than seeing a romantic interest's potential, focus on who they are at that moment.

With Venus in Virgo, you probably have an analytical approach to love. The more people you date, the more you know about what you want and don't want from a partner—information that you quietly store away. You are also able to look at romantic interests objectively; while you may have friends who start planning their wedding five dates in, you prefer to step back and consider whether a particular relationship really works in your life. You don't let your emotions stand in the way of your practical decision-making. Having good communication is key in a romantic relationship, and you appreciate when the other person plans a date far in advance and lets you know when, where, and how to show up. You are probably not super lovey-dovey or outwardly affectionate, though, instead demonstrating that you care by buying thoughtful gifts or doing small tasks to streamline your partner's life.

If you have Mars in Virgo, you are very methodical about what you put your energy and effort toward. You might be skilled at handling a lot of detailed information at once, and you could enjoy work that involves writing or sorting through data and numbers. Having a million things going on simultaneously helps to motivate you, and you may be an expert at thinking of last-minute solutions to any problems that arise. However, your love for fixing things may cause rifts in your relationships. When you get upset with your partner or a good friend, you may end up nagging and criticizing them or taking it upon yourself to fix their issues. You need to focus on what is actually within your control, such as your own reactions and behaviors in the relationship, rather than worrying so much about your partner's problems. When it comes to sexual intimacy, you may get turned on by pleasing the other person or by talking about what you both desire. It's just as necessary to have that open line of communication as it is to have physical touch and affection.

LIBRA VENUS AND MARS

Libra is the sign associated with romance and partnership. If you have your Venus or Mars in Libra, you enjoy being coupled up, and it is through your close relationships—both romantic and platonic— that you are better able to see the different sides of yourself and uncover where your talents lie. Other people offer you that necessary perspective, and you like being able to weigh your ideas against those of someone else before making big decisions. You're also naturally flirty and may always have a potential love interest that you're considering. Keeping the romance alive in a relationship is key for you, too, and you want a partner who will go out of their way to bring you breakfast in bed or buy you flowers or other thoughtful gifts. You're probably most attracted to people who have a good sense of style or who are well traveled and well versed in the arts and literature.

"I feel like I always have a crush on someone," says Julia, who has her Venus in Libra. However, she doesn't go for just anyone. "If I can't envision the person looking hot in a suit or presenting themselves well at a cocktail party for my work and knowing how to talk to people about cultured things, then that's really unattractive. I definitely overthink way into the future about how that person will appear next to me," she shares.

Similar to the other two air signs of Gemini and Aquarius, you are comfortable in social situations, but you probably prefer spending one-on-one time with people rather than hanging out in huge group settings. It's also easy for you to collaborate with others, because you are able to maintain balance and peace in all of your partnerships. You're very aware of the give-and-take that goes on in each relationship and how fairly each person is being treated, and you may make a conscious effort not to upset anyone. However, it is these same empathetic qualities that can lead to you being indecisive or staying in relationships longer than you should. There's a fear of hurting the other person's feelings, so you may actively avoid bringing up any issues or confronting your partner.

For those of you with Venus in Libra, you probably have a strong personal aesthetic. Venus rules the sign of Libra, and the qualities associated with this planet, such as an appreciation for art and beauty, can fully thrive in its home sign. You may have a love of film, fashion, music, or poetry, or be drawn to people who have a creative side themselves. In addition, having good manners is of the utmost importance to you. You may monitor the people you date, quickly weeding out anyone who isn't polite. You care about communicating well, so you could have this air of detachment at first when you're getting to know someone. Once in a relationship, though, you're a very thoughtful friend and partner who is always taking the needs of other people into consideration. Still, you may want to be wary of going too out of your way to make other people happy and neglecting what you really want.

Mars in Libra is almost an oxymoron, as Libra represents all of the qualities Mars is not. Mars is about taking immediate action, being assertive and independent, but when it falls in Libra, you may often look to other people for their opinions before you act on anything. You may not be entirely sure of your own instincts and value having someone else's feedback or reassurance first. Though you can be indecisive at times, you are at your best when putting your energy into building partnerships, and you may find that you accomplish more at work with the help of someone else. You're also a big proponent of people being treated fairly, which may cause you to be passionate about specific causes. When it comes to the physical aspect of a relationship, you may approach it in a polite, traditional way and might need a lot of romantic build-up with someone to feel excited. The biggest challenge you could face is in bringing up when something bothers you. You may have a fear of confrontation and don't want anyone to think poorly of you, but no one is going to know that you're upset if you don't tell them.

SCORPIO VENUS AND MARS

Scorpio is a sign that keeps its emotions heavily under wraps. If you have a Scorpio Mars or Venus, you may develop strong emotions quickly for the person you're interested in, but you're really good at keeping this side of yourself private. Oftentimes, a potential love interest may not even know you like them because of how secretive you can be with your feelings. You also tend to be pretty selective about who you let into your life, and, if there's not an immediate, intuitive sense of needing to know that person, you may not bother pursuing a relationship further.

Once you decide you like someone, your feelings can be all-consuming, and you may even have a tendency to get fixated on certain people. Your friends might call you obsessive or commend you on your detective skills; you like to figure out all there is to know about a particular person before you open your heart to them. The initial part of dating and getting to know someone may make you particularly anxious because you're not always in control. It may therefore take you a while to let your guard down and fully trust someone.

Julia has her Mars in Scorpio and describes her need to always have the upper hand in relationships. "With almost all of the guys I've been with, I've left them, because I like to be the one deciding when it ends." However, she admits that recently she was the one burned when she found out that the person she was seeing had been unfaithful. "Once I found that out, I never messaged him or talked to him again," she explains. "I don't want to give anyone the control to make me feel any sort of way." This takes us to our next point: when someone with a Scorpio Venus or Scorpio Mars placement feels betrayed within a relationship, they don't usually give second chances and they're done for good.

If you have your Venus in Scorpio, your approach when first dating someone may be to get deep pretty quickly. This can also go for friendships, too. You might find it hard to engage in surface-level connections, instead preferring to converse about topics pertaining to psychology, therapy, life, and death. If someone is not able to go there with you, you may think they aren't worth your time. Even outside of your love life, you're very black-and-white about who you want to associate with. Once you've let someone in, though, you're loyal to a fault. Developing greater trust within your relationships may be an area you need to work on, though. You might often be suspicious of people before you get to know them, or you frequently get jealous that the person you're dating is talking to other people. On a more positive note, relationships are probably the areas where you undergo the most transformation throughout your life. You may constantly be shedding old dating patterns in favor of developing healthier relationship habits. It may also be that you walk away from every romantic encounter having learned one major new aspect about yourself.

As for Mars in Scorpio, this is a placement that has a lot of tenacity. There may be a specific hobby or line of work that you are passionate about, and you're easily able to channel your energy into figuring out all there is to know about it. You may know exactly what goals you want to pursue, and you will go after them with intense determination and willpower. These same traits could be a bit problematic in your love life, though, and may result in controlling behavior toward your partner or an inability to let go of a relationship unless you have definitive answers or some sort of closure. Additionally, you may keep feelings of anger and frustration to yourself, until you reach a boiling point and they all come out at once. You could just expect other people to know that you're upset, even though you're very private about anything bothering you. Finally, when it comes to physical intimacy, you crave a lot of passion and intensity with your partner, and you may have strong sexual desires. Once again, though, this type of attraction will only occur with the right person, and it may be difficult to sleep with just anyone.

SAGITTARIUS VENUS AND MARS

Sagittarius is open-minded and has an adventurous spirit. If you have your Mars or Venus in this sign, you want to be inspired by whomever you're dating. You may often be attracted to people from foreign cultures or simply someone who has a different background or upbringing to you. Outside of relationships, you may put a lot of energy toward traveling, learning, reading, or writing. You have a constant thirst to obtain new knowledge and you may also have strong spiritual beliefs or other opinions that you proudly stand by. Even though you are someone who speaks about what you believe in with such strong conviction, you are still open to hearing from people who have a different outlook on life, as it often makes for an interesting conversation. In your relationships, you want to feel like you're being challenged and continually learning from your partner, and you love it when you can philosophize on the meaning of life or other bigger picture ideas together. Additionally, you might be pretty outgoing and social, or search for these traits in a partner and enjoy dating people who are funny or have a larger-than-life personality. You appreciate someone who is willing to explore and go on spontaneous adventures with you, without stressing out over last-minute details and planning. Anyone who is too rigid in their ways of thinking or not able to laugh at themselves from time to time probably isn't the best person for you.

You tend to look at life with a glass-half-full mentality, and even in difficult situations you may always try to find the important lesson. However, your inclination toward positive thinking may make it hard for you to open up and have tough conversations in your relationships. You also value your freedom, and the idea of settling down and committing to one person may seem scary to you. You don't want to miss out on anything going on with your friends, and you could fear that a partner would limit what you can and can't do. Rather than completely closing yourself off to developing intimacy with someone, you may just want to look for a partner who respects your need for independence and space.

"I like someone who is outside the norm," says Amelia, who has her Venus in Sagittarius. "I don't like to remain in one place, so I need someone who is going to follow me on trips, or just be down to go hiking with me the next day when I haven't planned anything out beforehand." Needy behavior or someone who needs constant reassurance is an immediate turn-off for her. "I love very freely. You need to know I love you, just as I trust that you love me."

Venus in Sagittarius is drawn to people who stand out for being different. In addition to romantic partners, you may be friends with people from all over the world. It is through your close relationships that you are better able to broaden your horizons and push yourself to try experiences outside of your comfort zone. When dating, you may quickly get super enthusiastic about a new person and could construct a fantasy of what it would be like to date them. You may have a habit of putting romantic interests on a pedestal and making them seem larger than life, so it may come as a shock when you are faced with the everyday realities of being in an actual relationship. Most people appreciate your optimistic spirit, though, and you might be the friend who is always encouraging other people to see their full potential and chase after their dreams. However, you will want to remain wary of being overly generous to others and giving too much of yourself away in your relationships.

If you have Mars in Sagittarius, in addition to most of the above, you can also be very honest and direct about what you want. If someone asks for your opinion, you usually tell it like it is. You can definitely be a bit blunt, which may rub people the wrong way sometimes. You need to make sure you're letting others get the chance to state their ideas or even disagree with you. Your energy may come and go in waves, and you could get the urge to act on your desires rather spontaneously. You have a need for adventure, and you may often feel restless inside if you don't have a trip to look forward to or a subject you're passionate about learning. What gets you the most excited in relationships might be having conversations that go on for hours, where you discuss your beliefs or visions for the future and are able to connect on a mental level.

CAPRICORN VENUS AND MARS

Capricorn takes commitment very seriously. If you have your Venus or Mars in this sign, you might be cautious about who you choose to date and don't enter into relationships lightly. You may not experience as many flings or situationships as some of your friends do, but when you are with someone, it's more likely that it will last a long time. You view relationships as carrying a lot of duty and responsibility, so you put careful thought into what type of partner you want to be with, and there usually has to be long-term potential with someone for you to give them your attention. You're probably drawn to people who are ambitious and independent, or who have already established themselves within their careers. It may even be that relationships and work go hand in hand, where you're either drawn to people who work in your same field, or you literally end up establishing a business relationship with a romantic partner.

You may still be a bit reserved when first getting to know someone. You might get criticized for being unemotional or overly serious, even if you don't feel this way inside. You just happen to be more controlled about the emotions you decide to share. You probably attract partners who act similarly, and you appreciate when someone comes across as poised and mature. A huge turn-off for you would be anyone who is too loud and rambunctious or all over the place with their emotions. It's important that you scope out this type of behavior early on, and you may hold people at arm's length until they have proven themselves to you.

"I liked that he was well-spoken, well-traveled, and knew several different languages. Being in his company made me feel like I was learning something," says Nora, who has her Mars in Capricorn, about a previous person she dated. "In comparison, I would go out with guys who didn't know how to order a glass of wine. That to me is just so unattractive. I need someone who knows how to handle themselves, is cool under pressure, knows what's going on, and is very structured and serious."

For those with their Venus in Capricorn, you may choose partners who are older, more established, or who have an air of authority. Ideally, you want someone you look up to, and who you are excited to show off to your friends and family. It could also be that the people you end up with elevate your social status. You may go about dating in a traditional way, so casual hook-ups or undefined situationships won't be that appealing to you. When you're seeing someone, you want to define the relationship early on in order to figure out if it's going anywhere—it may make you anxious not knowing where you stand. On the other hand, your career is of utmost importance to you, so you could hold off on looking for a serious relationship until you feel like you're in a comfortable place professionally and financially.

Mars in Capricorn is just as ambitious and goal-oriented, and those with this placement usually have a strong desire to achieve something of importance or rise to a position of authority at work. You need to feel like you're working toward a set of concrete goals. However, it could take time to pinpoint exactly what you want to put your energy into, and you may doubt your natural instincts. With physical intimacy, you may first need to feel secure within a relationship before you can feel truly comfortable. You take pride in being independent, and it may scare you to be put in a vulnerable position with someone or have to depend on others for anything. It might also be that having sex is not a huge priority for you, and you're able to hold off for long periods of time until you meet the right person.

Oftentimes, with either Venus or Mars in Capricorn, you may end up finding greater success with love and dating as you get older. You might initially experience low self-esteem in this area of your life, and you could struggle to be your authentic self when dating or even find it hard to let on that you like the other person for fear of rejection. You may also attract partners who are overly critical or controlling of you, or you could be the one who is constantly calling out the other person's flaws. As time goes on and you become more comfortable in your own skin, you will inevitably shed any self-imposed limitations you put on yourself when dating, finding that it's much easier to form meaningful relationships.

AQUARIUS VENUS AND MARS

Aquarius is known for its desire to be different. If you have your Venus or Mars in this sign, you probably take an unconventional approach to dating. You might be drawn to relationships that are outside of the norm, like having a long-distance relationship, experimenting with non-monogamy, or simply not seeing the point in getting married and following the status quo when it comes to dating rules. You tend to go against tradition and societal expectations of what a relationship should look like. A need for a certain degree of independence and space carries over into your friendships and love life, too. You probably have a wide network of acquaintances from all different walks of life but are likely the type of person who doesn't need to be in contact with your friends every day to maintain a relationship. You like to have a detached distance from people, which works well for making friends online or through social media. You don't like to be tied down to one specific group, and you're typically drawn to eccentric people who either do something unique for work or who live a different type of lifestyle.

You also have the ability to come up with innovative ideas that no one else has yet considered, and you may often think about the future for both you personally and society at large. You probably love talking about your desire to change the world with a community of like-minded people, or you could be the most engaged in conversations where you're discussing kind of "out there" topics that other people may find weird. However, you may not be as articulate when discussing your feelings with a love interest. Although you thrive in bigger social settings, having emotionally charged one-on-one conversations may be a bit uncomfortable for you—it could even feel like it's more difficult for you than it is for others to show public affection or be vulnerable. When you like someone, your initial instinct may even be to act like they don't exist, and you could come across as aloof or untouchable.

Lindsey, who has her Venus in Aquarius, shares that she often gets feedback from the people she's closest to, like her past boyfriends or her best friends, saying that they feel like she doesn't care about them. She was initially confused, because in her mind these were people that she deeply loved. Over time she realized that the way she shows she cares is by sharing information and observations with them, rather than being warm and fuzzy. "If I love someone and they have a problem, I want to help them solve the problem. I'll be shamelessly honest and forthright with them, but I only do that with the people that I love. I often forget the importance of telling someone how much they mean to me, giving them words of affirmation or just being less intense in general."

Venus in Aquarius has very original tastes. Not one to follow trends, you may like to dress in clothing that no one else owns or you actively avoid traveling to places that you see all over Instagram. You may also have a few solo hobbies you like to pursue in your free time—having space to do your own thing is a must. When it comes to romantic partners and friends, you may like to keep your distance at first or be less forthcoming with your emotions, as you want to analyze a person and get a read on who they really are. You may also have a fear that your independence will be compromised or that you will be controlled by someone else if you're in a relationship. On the other hand, it might be flipped, where you end up attracting people who are non-committal or who avoid telling you how they feel about you. An ideal relationship scenario for you is when you and your partner are on the same page about having both time together and moments apart.

Mars in Aquarius is the most motivated by planning for the future or discussing big ideas with people. You may put your energy toward humanitarian causes, and you're also skilled at networking and bringing people together for a specific purpose. Your energy levels may be a bit unpredictable, though, coming and going in spurts, or you may like to go against the grain and be different just for the sake of being different. You could have a pattern of rebelling against authority figures, and you may get worked up about societal structures that are dated and need to be reworked. You tend to be more turned on by ideas and stimulating conversations than you are by physical intimacy, and it could be difficult to tap into your sensual side or be present in your body when you're with someone.

PISCES VENUS AND MARS

Pisces is often referred to as a hopeless romantic. If you have your Venus or Mars in this sign, you may have the desire to fall head over heels in love, and, even though you may not readily admit it, you like it when your partner goes out of their way to plan something romantic. You also have a lot of kindness and compassion for other people, and you're easily able to empathize with someone and understand what they might be going through. At times, though, you may be overly giving to others, especially to the people you're romantically interested in. You may go out of your way to fix your partner's problems, or you could be someone who drops everything you're doing when the person you like texts you, asking to hang out. Once you've developed feelings for a person, it may be like you're wearing rose-tinted glasses, and you could have to be extra wary of overlooking any major red flags or building up too much of a fantasy around what you want the relationship to look like. You don't want to lose your sense of self, especially if you're only just getting to know someone.

"I was so caught up in the idea of him being this cool person and me wanting that same image for myself out of insecurity," Olivia, who has Mars in Pisces, says about her past relationship. "I was going into his world and living through him instead of having my own life, which was ultimately really hard for me when it ended, because I was kicked out of this whole fantasy that I had." Because Mars and Venus in Pisces are both placements that may end up overly romanticizing their relationships, oftentimes without even knowing who the person really is, it can be especially difficult when a break-up occurs and that dream is shattered. You may need to stop and consider whether you even like the other person before you spend so much time envisioning a future together.

With Venus in Pisces, you may have an interest in the arts and fashion, and you probably have a very distinct aesthetic. In addition, you may like to immerse yourself in learning about spirituality, manifestation, or other forms of mysticism, and you could even have natural healing qualities that you end up incorporating into your job. It's not uncommon for people with this placement to end up in a line of work that helps other people, because Pisces likes to feel like there's always a deeper meaning behind what they do. When dating, you may need a partner who appreciates how sensitive and caring you are, rather than taking advantage of these traits. You like it when the person you're seeing goes out of their way to bring you flowers, write you love letters, or organize romantic dates.

You put just as much effort, if not more, into your relationships as well, and you may end up selflessly giving to your partner. There could also be an element of escapism in your relationships, where you end up taking on the other person's interests or looking to your partner too much to give you a sense of identity. Developing your own passions and hobbies is key before you can commit to someone else.

Having Mars in Pisces is very similar to all of the above. You like to put your efforts into artistic or spiritual endeavors, but your energy may come in short spurts, or you may only be motivated to do something if there is a greater purpose behind it. For example, Olivia, who spoke about her Mars in Pisces placement earlier, works in fashion and, in her free time, writes creative poetry and studies astrology. Finding some sort of outlet where you give back to other people may be necessary as well. However, your work ethic may not be super consistent, and you may often daydream about what you will one day accomplish instead of putting in the mundane work to get there. Establishing everyday rituals or making to-do lists may help you to feel more grounded. You could also be a bit indirect about what you desire out of a relationship or with sex, expecting the other person to be able to read your mind. It may be that you're not totally confident in acting on what you want, and you like to have time to feel out a situation first and reflect on it. With experience, you may find it easier to trust your strong emotions and intuition.

The aspects are indicated by the lines
running through your birth chart.

CHAPTER 7

How the Planets Relate: Aspects

Now that we've gone over your moon, Venus, and Mars signs in depth, we can go one step further in understanding how they may show up for you. What we are about to get into now is quite technical, so if you need to pause before moving on and let what you've just learned soak in a little bit, feel free to do so.

From time to time, I get people messaging me asking why they don't entirely resonate with their moon, Venus, or Mars signs. For example, I've spoken with several people who have Capricorn moons who say that they don't really identify with being super responsible or guarded with their emotions. Rather, they feel quite sensitive and emotional a lot of the time. Just as I've suspected, when I've pulled up each of their birth charts, I've seen that their Capricorn moon falls right next to Neptune. Enter the aspects, which are the various lines that run through your birth chart, shown in the diagram opposite. Aspects indicate how the various planets are interacting with each other and how the traits associated with one planet may end up influencing the characteristics of another. In the example I just mentioned, we would say in astrological speak that the moon in Capricorn is in an aspect to Neptune. Aspects can look complicated at first glance, but when they're broken down, they are much easier to understand.

To ground the concept of aspects in another example, let's take two different people's charts that both happen to have their moon in Pisces. One person's moon and Saturn are in an aspect to one another, while the other person's moon is in an aspect to Jupiter. The Saturn–moon person may be very emotionally mature, having taken on a lot of responsibilities (Saturn) at home (moon) from a young age. They may also be a bit guarded (Saturn) with their feelings (moon), finding it difficult to open up to others, and they could come across as very serious. By contrast, the Jupiter–moon person may have had a very different experience at home. They might feel very supported (Jupiter) by their family (moon), and they might be generous (Jupiter) in sharing their feelings (moon) with people. Rather than being guarded, they may wear their emotions on their sleeve, feeling every high and low very intensely. Even though these two people have the same Pisces moon sign, how they express that moon will be vastly different based on what aspects the moon is making to other planets in their chart.

DEGREES

We haven't yet learned about the degrees in your chart, but they become especially relevant in the context of aspects. If you are looking at your birth chart, you may notice numbers located next to each planet. These numbers represent the degree of the sign at which the planet is placed. Within each sign of the zodiac, there are 30 degrees, so the number next to a planet can never be higher than 29. You see the degrees marked as the little notch marks that line the edge of the signs in your chart. For a visual, take a look at the diagram on page 86.

When we get into the various aspects, you will want to prioritize the aspects in your chart that are closest in degree. For example, if you notice that two planets are in a conjunction, with one planet being at 20 degrees of Aquarius and the other being at 21 degrees of Aquarius, that conjunction would be exact, because the two planets are only one degree apart. On the other hand, if one planet is at 20 degrees of Aquarius while the other is at 29 degrees of Aquarius, that would also still be considered a conjunction, but it's not as exact and will not be felt quite as intensely. As you learn about the aspects, take note of which aspects in your chart are closest by degree. Exact aspects are when two planets are within five degrees of one another, while wider aspects can be up to 10 degrees apart. If this seems a bit complicated, first focus on familiarizing yourself with the aspects below, and then come back to learning about degrees to take your knowledge one step further.

There are many aspects that show up in astrology, but I only use the five major ones listed below.

WHEN PLANETS BLEND TOGETHER: Conjunction

A conjunction occurs when two planets are touching in the same sign and house or are within 10 degrees of one another. In the diagram at the start of this chapter, you can see that Mars and Jupiter are in a conjunction because they are located closely together in the sign of Libra. When this aspect occurs, the qualities of the two planets blend together, and it may sometimes be difficult to differentiate between the two of them, because they act as one. The conjunction is neither good nor bad, as it really depends on what two planets are involved. A Venus–Jupiter conjunction, which would symbolize good fortune, financial abundance, and positive growth within friendships and romantic relationships, is going to be much easier to handle than a Mars–Saturn conjunction, which would concern strenuous effort, overcoming obstacles, or experiencing difficulty in expressing anger or frustration.

WHEN PLANETS ARE IN CONFLICT: Square

A square occurs when two planets are at a 90-degree angle from one another and are located three signs apart. Referring back to the diagram on page 86, there is a square between Venus in Leo and Pluto in Scorpio. There is also another square between both Jupiter and Mars in Libra to Neptune and Uranus in Capricorn. Within a square, there is a lot of tension that occurs between the two planets, and it represents two parts of yourself that are constantly clashing against each other. The square can be very activating, and significant personal growth will often occur because of the internal frustration this aspect causes. You will often feel like you need to actively work on integrating the energy of both of these planets into your life.

WHEN PLANETS ARE IN A BALANCING ACT: Opposition
An opposition occurs when two planets are opposing one another or are 180 degrees apart. In the diagram, Venus in Leo and Saturn in Aquarius are in an opposition. You can think of an opposition as a seesaw, where you're trying to balance the energies of both planets and integrate them into your life. However, one of the planets in the opposition may come more naturally to you, while you may end up projecting the qualities associated with the other planet onto other people. Relationships may help you to better develop that planet and side of yourself.

WHEN PLANETS SUPPORT ONE ANOTHER: Trine
A trine forms when two planets are 120 degrees apart and connects two planets that are in the same element. In the diagram, the sun in earth sign Virgo forms a trine to both Neptune and Uranus in earth sign Capricorn. Jupiter and Mars in Libra also trine Saturn in Aquarius. Two planets in a trine can easily work together and will often show a skill or natural gift that you have. Because the trine is so easy going though, it typically doesn't promote a lot of growth or the desire to work on yourself, or you may end up taking that particular skill for granted. You might have to push yourself to incorporate the energies of the two planets more fully into your life.

WHEN PLANETS COMPLEMENT EACH OTHER: Sextile

A sextile occurs when two planets are 60 degrees apart. The two planets connected by a sextile are in elements that are compatible with one another, so fire sign planets are sextile to air sign planets, while water sign planets are sextile to earth sign planets. In the diagram, the moon in Leo sextiles Mercury in Libra. Venus in Leo also sextiles Mars and Jupiter in Libra. There is a blend of fire and air signs in both examples. There is also a sextile between the sun in Virgo and Pluto in Scorpio—an earth and a water sign. The sextile is similar to the trine, in that the two planets are supportive of one another and can easily work together when they are connected. The trine brings out the more positive signification of the two planets involved.

To identify what aspects are happening between the moon, Venus, and Mars in your birth chart, let's go through the following steps together. Understanding how to locate aspects and what they mean can feel confusing at first, so bear with me.

How to identify your aspects

1. **IF YOU ARE USING ASTRO.COM TO LOOK AT YOUR BIRTH CHART, YOU WILL SEE A TRIANGLE-SHAPED GRID AT THE BOTTOM OF YOUR CHART, LIKE THE IMAGE ON THE NEXT PAGE.** From there, you can run your finger down the column of each planetary symbol to see where it intersects with the row of another planet. For now, ignore the number and the letter next to the aspect symbols, as well as any symbols that were not included above. If you are using astro-seek.com for this exercise, it makes your life a whole lot easier by simply listing what aspects each planet makes if you keep scrolling down below your chart.

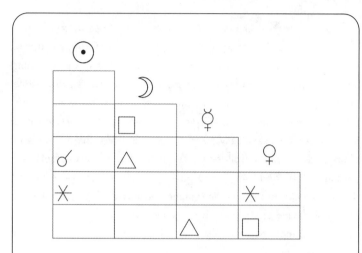

2. **IF AN ASPECT EXISTS BETWEEN TWO PLANETS, YOU WILL SEE ONE OF THE ASPECT SYMBOLS WE JUST WENT OVER AT THE POINT OF INTERSECTION.** In the image above, you can see that the triangle symbol for the trine is located at the point where the rows for the moon and Venus meet. So, in this chart, we would say that the moon and Venus are trining each other.

3. **GO OVER THIS EXERCISE THREE TIMES: ONCE FOR YOUR MOON, THEN FOR VENUS, AND FINALLY FOR MARS.** Before you read on, you may want to write down the aspects each of these planets make with both the other planets in your chart and with each other.

Let's finally jump into what exactly these aspects mean. In the following examples, when I describe the moon, Venus, or Mars as "making an aspect" to each of these planets, I'm referring to all of the five major aspects we just went over: the conjunction, trine, sextile, square, or opposition. If you have an opposition or square between two planets, you may find it challenging for those planets to cooperate, and you could face repeated lessons in incorporating them into your life. Meanwhile, if you have a trine or sextile for any of the planetary combinations mentioned, you will feel the positive effects of those two planets more easily, and it won't be an area that weighs on you as much. In addition, aspects between two planets go both ways. Finally, keep in mind that your moon, Venus, and Mars are probably going to make aspects to more than one planet, so several of these explanations will apply to you. It may take a while to fully get comfortable with identifying aspects in your chart, but try to go through each planet and make notes on the aspects it makes.

ASPECTS WITH THE SUN

The sun is your core identity, so when Venus, the moon, or Mars aspect the sun, the flavor of that particular planet informs your sense of who you are. With a **sun–Venus aspect**, for instance, you may thrive in partnerships, and your close relationships help you to better understand yourself. You might always be dating someone or be popular within your group of friends. You give off an approachable, friendly energy and you're able to maintain balance with the people in your life. You're very aware of the give and take in your relationships, and you don't like to see other people upset. If we're talking about **sun–Mars aspects**, you will be a bit fierier and more impulsive. You like to act immediately on your desires, and you may be confident in initiating the first move with someone. However, you may be a bit hot-headed or impatient with other people at times, or you could jump into relationships quickly without considering if you truly like the person.

Sun–moon aspects are a little different. The interplay between the sun and moon speaks to how you process your emotions, and how you strike a balance between your head and your heart. It can also say something about the early home environment, whether it was nurturing or tense. I want to zero in on the hard aspects between the sun and moon specifically. An aspect like the square may mean that there was relationship conflict at home or a feeling of being misunderstood by your family. You may have to work harder as an adult to fulfill your emotional needs and make sure you're listening to your intuitive voice as much as your logical one. Meanwhile, people born with the sun–moon opposition are relationship people, and they are better able to understand their own feelings by closely interacting with another person. Their relationships reflect back what is still undeveloped within themselves. Finally, the closer you are born to the sun–moon conjunction, the more self-focused you will be: sometimes you could find yourself so concerned with your own emotions that it's hard to step outside of yourself and consider another person. A great book on diving deeper into the relationship between the sun and moon in your chart can be found in *Aspects in Astrology* (1989) by Sue Tompkins.

ASPECTS WITH THE MOON

If Mars or Venus aspect your moon, this will influence how you process and express your emotions. These two planets are very different, though. **Venus in aspect to the moon** will be calm and nurturing. It might be easy for you to share affection and love with others, and you bring a distinctly maternal quality to both your friendships and romantic relationships. You're very aware of how other people are feeling and are able to establish a sense of peace and balance in your relationships. However, you may feel uncomfortable expressing feelings of upset or frustration, as you don't want to come across as impolite. You may be too concerned with what other people might think of you if you were to show how you really felt.

Mars aspects to the moon are the complete opposite: they give your emotions a passionate, fiery quality. You may have the tendency to get upset quickly and fire back responses in the heat of the moment. Sometimes it may feel like your blood is literally boiling when you're frustrated with someone. Your emotions very much guide your actions, so when you feel strongly about a situation, you may react impulsively or snap at people. You don't tiptoe around conflict. You're very upfront and direct, and the people close to you never have to guess why you're upset. However, it's important to put yourself in your partner's shoes, because sometimes the way you express your feelings can come off as aggressive.

ASPECTS WITH MERCURY

Aspects between Venus, the moon, or Mars and Mercury give you natural social skills, and having someone with whom communication flows naturally is a priority in your relationships. You love to talk to people, and you need a regular back-and-forth conversation with a love interest or a good friend to feel satisfied. You may also have a natural ability to write well or speak eloquently, so you could look for people who are smart and witty like you. It may feel like your thoughts are always racing, though, and you have to make an effort when putting your mind toward some type of productive activity. Deciding what topics to focus on in depth or what tasks you want to channel your energy into may constantly be evolving, and your feelings toward people may change just as quickly. It could be difficult to decide on one person to settle down with in a committed relationship, and you may often wonder what else is out there. You will know you're with the right person when your racing thoughts at last settle down.

ASPECTS WITH VENUS

Moon–Venus and Mercury–Venus aspects are mentioned above. If Mars makes an aspect to Venus in your chart, though, you may grow impatient with the process of dating or you're always eager to move onto the next phase of a relationship. You can be quite direct about who and what you like, and when you're attracted to someone you may wish that things would just happen already. You might be proactive about putting yourself out there and mingling with new people. Additionally, you may be drawn to partners who are equally as assertive, or there could be a competitive nature in a few of your close relationships. Relationships energize you, and you may be motivated by the prospect of teaming up with someone and sharing your life with them. You have a lot of passion and intensity that you need to direct somewhere. You may want to be wary of jumping into relationships too quickly, though, and could experience a pattern of moving fast with someone early on only to have it fizzle out shortly after.

ASPECTS WITH MARS

Moon–Mars aspects are mentioned under the moon, and **Venus–Mars aspects** are mentioned under Venus.

ASPECTS WITH JUPITER

If you have your **moon, Venus, or Mars in an aspect to Jupiter**, you enter into relationships with a lot of optimism, and you could get easily excited about a potential future with someone. You might be a naturally outgoing and friendly person, and you have a fun, relaxed disposition that other people like to be around. When dating, you might be drawn to people from different cultures or will want a partner who you can learn from. You're also very generous to your friends and romantic interests, but you could end up giving too much of yourself away to others, going out of your way to do things for other people, or making grand promises you can't always keep. You may have difficulty knowing when to set a boundary and take necessary time to tend to your own needs. In addition, you might experience a whole spectrum of feelings regularly, especially if your moon is in an aspect to Jupiter. There is no calm middle ground for you, and you could end up with frequent emotional highs and lows.

ASPECTS WITH SATURN

If you have your **moon, Venus, or Mars in an aspect to Saturn**, you keep your emotions under control. When you're first getting to know someone, you may be guarded or find it hard to be vulnerable and ask for help from people. You are used to being the responsible one among your friends and family, and you never want to appear needy or weak. Your desire to be so self-sufficient can sometimes prevent you from forming more intimate connections with people. Not a fan of casual situationships, you like to know where you stand in your relationships at all times. You may only entertain people who have long-term potential, and you crave having a sense of structure and stability with your partner. You probably like to date people who are older than you, have their life together, or who can somehow elevate your status. However, you may also have a tendency to be very critical toward both yourself and your romantic partners. With age and maturity, you are learning how to stop putting yourself down so much or how to avoid always assuming the worst when dating.

ASPECTS WITH URANUS

If your **moon, Venus, or Mars is in an aspect to Uranus**, you like to maintain your independence when you're in a relationship. You might be drawn to relationships that give you that necessary space, like a long-distance relationship or having an open relationship. You like to be free to do as you want without feeling like anyone is trying to control you. You march to the beat of your own drum when dating, and you don't really follow specific dating rules or adhere to what society thinks a relationship should look like. Additionally, you may like a partner who will do things to surprise you, like planning spontaneous trips or being open-minded to trying out different experiences. You never want to fall into the same old routine with someone. Switching things up in other areas of your life is just as necessary, and you may not like being tied down to living in one city or hanging out with one sole group of people. However, your actions can at times be chaotic, and your feelings for people may run hot and cold as well. You could often come across as detached or unemotional, but you're just not a super affectionate person.

ASPECTS WITH NEPTUNE

If you have your **moon, Venus, or Mars in an aspect to Neptune**, you are probably extra sensitive to other people's energy. Your intuition is strong, but your feelings may be overwhelming at times, and you could take on other people's pain or bad moods. However, it's these same qualities that make you a compassionate person who can easily empathize with others and offer up helpful insight. You may go out of your way to do nice things for people, especially those whom you're romantically interested in, but sometimes it may be like you're wearing rose-tinted glasses when dating; you only see what you want to see in a person, not wanting to face the reality of a relationship. There may be a desire to form a deep bond with your partner to feel like you're meeting on a soul-to-soul level, but be wary of losing your sense of self along the way. You could also feel bad about hurting a person's feelings, which makes it difficult for you to stand up for yourself and set boundaries in your close relationships.

ASPECTS WITH PLUTO

If your **moon, Venus, or Mars is in an aspect to Pluto**, what people see of you on the surface level is only the tip of the iceberg. You like your privacy and may be secretive about your emotions. You tend to be super selective about who you date and choose to open up to, but when you do like someone you usually have pretty intense feelings for that person that can sometimes border on obsession.

If you're interested in a person, it might be difficult for you to keep things casual—you like going deep quickly. In both your romantic relationships and your friendships, you may enjoy discussing taboo topics or diving into someone's past and talking about their problems. However, you may find it hard to trust people, or you could have some jealous tendencies. You may get fixated on having a specific outcome happen with someone, or you could have a fear of not being in control. On a more positive note, relationships are a big point of transformation for you, where you're continually made aware of certain patterns that you need to heal or release from.

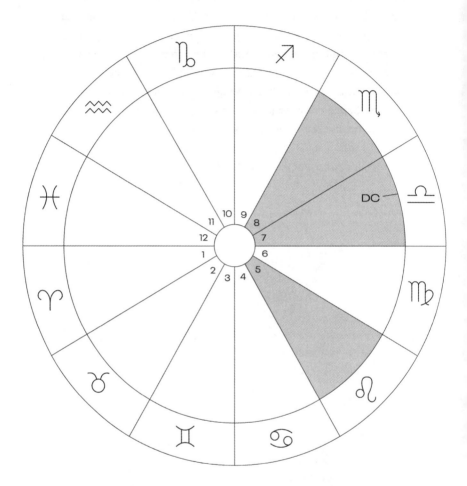

Houses linked to relationships are shaded in the diagram.
The descendant is always in the seventh house.

CHAPTER 8

Where Your Love Life Is the Focus: Relationship Houses

For the final component in looking at your own birth chart through the lens of relationships, we can't forget the houses. We've covered a lot of astrology already, and every chapter we've gone through has been building upon the previous, helping you to put together a fuller and more nuanced picture of how you approach dating and relationships. Think of the houses as that last layer that ties everything together. As mentioned in the introduction, the houses pertain to specific areas of life. For the fifth, seventh, and eighth houses, intimate relationship matters are the focus.

It's so important to look at each of these houses on their own. We talk so often about the planets and signs and how they shape our personalities, but the houses are just as crucial in understanding your chart. Even if you don't have any planets located in the fifth, seventh, or eighth houses, there will still be a sign that rules each house and a ruling planet associated with that sign, which will influence how you experience relationships. So, before you say that you're doomed in love because these houses are "empty" for you, read this entire chapter first! In addition, when we get to Part Four on timing relationship activity, you will learn that one of these three houses is almost always activated when a significant relationship event takes place, so try to keep the meaning of each house stored in the back of your mind for now.

Building Greater
Self-Confidence: The Fifth House

THE FIFTH HOUSE is concerned with romance, but first and foremost it has to do with self-esteem. It sheds light on how much you value the traits that make you unique and how comfortable you are expressing your full personality when you are around other people. This mindset factors in your love life because it indicates how you may act when entertaining a new romantic interest, as well as how high or low your dating standards might be. It can be hard to attract a partner who loves and respects you when you are constantly criticizing yourself or believing that no one better will ever come along for you. Therefore, mastering self-love and self-confidence starts in the fifth house. On a lighter note, the fifth house is associated with hobbies and games, so it often points to the more playful side of dating, when you're first getting to know someone. It describes your approach to physical affection, and it also embodies the traits you find to be sexually attractive in another person. Finally, the fifth has to do with children and pregnancy, creative hobbies, or even passion projects that you feel like you've given birth to, but we're not going to get into that side as much here.

Planets placed in the fifth house (if you have any) and the sign ruling this house in your chart will speak to how you express all of the themes mentioned above. Having a planet like Saturn in your fifth house or Capricorn as the sign ruling it may mean that you can be very self-critical or afraid to share your feelings for fear of getting rejected. It may be hard for you to let loose and have fun in social situations or when dating. In contrast, having the sun placed in this house or Leo as the sign ruling it may mean that you bring a lot of passion to dating, and you may feel like having a variety of dating experiences helps to shape your identity and further discover who you are. If you're someone who has multiple planets in the fifth house, then there's an extra emphasis in your life on learning how to be more confident, leaning into your creative skills, and being comfortable sticking up for yourself or expressing your true feelings to the people you like.

Establishing Commitment:
The Seventh House and the Descendant

WHEREAS THE FIFTH house can be thought of as the fun, romantic side of relationships during that period when you're first getting to know someone, the seventh house is more about establishing commitment and actually putting in effort to be one half of a partnership. Planets placed within the seventh and the sign ruling your seventh speak to what you're looking for in a long-term partner, how you relate to other people on a one-on-one level, as well as patterns that you may attract in your relationships. In addition to romantic relationships, the seventh house also covers business partnerships and your closest friendships, and how you achieve balance between you and another person.

Planets placed in the seventh house, as well as the sign ruling this house in your chart, will point to how you approach these close interactions with people. For example, if you have Venus in your seventh house, you may be good at achieving balance in your relationships and taking someone else into consideration. You like to maintain the peace with people in your life, but that may also mean it's difficult for you to bring up problems or show that you're upset with someone. By contrast, having Pluto in your seventh house means that you may struggle with needing to be in control in your close relationships, or you could be very selective about who you commit to. You may not experience as many flings or shorter relationships as your friends do, but when you are with someone, it's usually for the long haul.

We can't talk about the seventh house without mentioning the descendant (DC), which is one of the four angles in your chart. The descendant always falls opposite your ascendant (AC, also known as your rising sign). Your ascendant is the part of yourself that you feel comfortable showing off and expressing to the world, while the descendant indicates traits that are often lying dormant within you and which often get reflected back to you by a partner. It is through having close relationships that you are shown the sides of yourself that you need to further develop, rather than projecting these traits onto other people. To give a concrete example here, you may notice that you experience a similar situation over and over again in your romantic relationships. No matter who the person is, there's always the same underlying theme. Maybe you attract people who move super quickly in the beginning, but then a few weeks in suddenly grow distant, or it could be that you feel like you're always having to parent the people you date and take care of all of their problems. In both of these situations your partners are acting as mirrors, by showing you what parts of yourself you need to recognize and fully embrace. In the case of the person who keeps dating people who suddenly pull away, maybe they need to become more comfortable being independent and taking time to have space and be by themselves. Meanwhile, the person who constantly feels like they have to mother the people they date may want to look into ways they can better nurture themself.

I want you now to locate the sign in which your ascendant is placed, which is also known as your rising sign. With your birth chart in front of you, move your eye to the sign exactly opposite your ascendant. On astro-seek.com, there should be a line labelled DC (or DSC), but if you're using astro.com, you will simply see a bold notch marking the spot. You can also refer back to the diagram at the start of this chapter to see approximately where the DC will be. As you're reading about your descendant over the next few pages, reflect on whether any of your romantic partners or closest friends embody the traits associated with that particular sign. They may even have that sign as their sun, moon, or rising as well.

ARIES RISING » LIBRA DESCENDANT

As an Aries rising, you probably come across as independent and full of energy. You are comfortable prioritizing yourself and your own goals, and you like to take action and get things done immediately.

However, you can sometimes be a bit impatient or brusque with people who don't move at your same pace. With a Libra descendant, you may attract partners who are the complete opposite. They like to make sure everyone else is okay and being treated fairly, and other people may find them to be polite and charming. You may also admire the people you date for their sense of style and how cultured they are. However, you could sometimes feel like your partners are almost too accommodating and get frustrated when they don't speak up for themselves or are too dependent on you to make all the decisions. You might also attract people who want immediate commitment, but you're a bit hesitant because you don't want your independence to be compromised. It is through your close relationships that you are learning how to work as part of a team and consider others, instead of prioritizing your own wants and needs all of the time. When you become comfortable with leaning on other people for support, you will probably stop attracting people who are overly needy.

TAURUS RISING » SCORPIO DESCENDANT

As a Taurus rising, you may come across as well dressed and put together. You have good taste, and probably a deep appreciation for the arts, beauty, and fashion. Your interactions with people tend to be very patient and refined, and you put careful thought into how you respond. Additionally, you tend to approach life in a practical, level-headed way, not usually making impulsive decisions or being dramatic in how you express your emotions. However, your Scorpio descendant means that you may end up in relationships that are all-consuming, with a lot of passion and intensity. In addition, your interactions with romantic partners and close friends may often bring up feelings of jealousy or trust issues. You could have a fear of not being in control in your relationships or, on the flip side, you may end up with people who are overly controlling toward you. Instead of focusing so much on the surface level—trying to look good for other people and not rock the boat—your relationships are here to teach you to be more comfortable with exploring your own emotions and anything else you may keep repressed. When you lean into these more complicated feelings, your relationships will be less about fighting for control and more about undergoing positive change and transformation with your partner.

GEMINI RISING » SAGITTARIUS DESCENDANT

As a Gemini rising, you come across as friendly and approachable. You enjoy connecting with many different kinds of people, and you're skilled at navigating small talk and coming up with interesting topics. Additionally, you enjoy having your hand in a variety of projects at once and may like to keep your mind occupied with reading, writing, or coming up with social media content. However, you may find it difficult to settle down and go in depth on one particular subject, and your opinions might be constantly changing. With a Sagittarius descendant, you are naturally drawn to people who have an extensive knowledge of the world and with whom you can learn from. They may also be super adventurous or come from a different cultural background from your own. You may envy their innate optimism and ability to step back and look at the bigger picture in life. However, your partners or good friends may have strong opinions that they assert over yours, and they may think that they are always right. Instead of relying on someone else to give you their wisdom, you have to trust that you have it inside of yourself, too. Once you stop fixating on petty gossip or obsessing over small, everyday details, you will come to realize that you don't need a free-spirited partner to complete you, and that you may actually have those same qualities within yourself.

CANCER RISING » CAPRICORN DESCENDANT

As a Cancer rising, it may take some time for you to warm up to new people, and you could be a bit shy at first. You also have strong maternal instincts and may be easily able to sense other people's emotions, and you enjoy building others up by offering your advice and support. In addition, you might have a strong bond with your family and the place where you grew up. Creating a stable home life for yourself might also be a priority. Your feelings may fluctuate a lot, though: you could feel on top of the world one day but be sad the next. With a Capricorn descendant, you may look to the people you date to be a rock for your emotions. You're probably attracted to partners who are well respected and ambitious, or you might like being around people who are older, responsible, and serious. However, you may often end up in relationships where the other person is always the one in charge, or you could date people who aren't as forthcoming about their emotions and who can be cold and distant from time to time. You may also feel like their achievements always overshadow your own, or that they are very critical of your shortcomings. The challenge in your relationships is to tap into your inner authority and develop your own ambitions, instead of always championing someone else's success. When you are able to do that, you will experience relationships where the other person supports you just as much as you support them.

LEO RISING » AQUARIUS DESCENDANT

As a Leo rising, you have a playful spirit and childlike approach to life, and you're always coming up with ways to be creative and have fun. You bring a lot of passion to the relationships, work, and hobbies that you care about, and you also give off a warm, heartfelt energy. However, you can also be particularly self-conscious and a little too concerned with what other people think about you. With an Aquarius descendant, you might be drawn to partners who go against the status quo and are comfortable with the ways in which they are different. You may like how they don't seem to care as much as you do, and secretly you may wish that you could be as cool and detached as they are. However, you may attract people who are also emotionally distant or hot and cold with their feelings for you. They may keep you guessing, and it could feel like you're always trying to win their approval and get them to notice you. Once you embrace your quirks and stop looking for other people to validate you, you will no longer be interested in chasing after people who just don't care. A healthy relationship is one where you are both able to find moments of alone time, rather than the other person giving you too much space and leaving you hanging.

VIRGO RISING » PISCES DESCENDANT

As a Virgo rising, you have an eye for detail, and you like having structure and routine in your everyday life. You're always looking for ways to improve upon yourself, whether that be through taking care of your physical body or continually striving to work harder. You want to feel like you're putting your skills to use and being productive in some way, but you can also be very critical and hard on yourself. With a Pisces descendant, you may frequently be drawn to people who are sensitive, artistic, and in touch with their emotions. It is through your close relationships that you are learning how to be more compassionate toward yourself and others. However, you may be prone to overly romanticizing your relationships, and you only see what you want to see about the other person, often ignoring red flags or building up a fantasy around what your future could look like with them. You may also attract people who have emotional problems that you end up taking on and making your own responsibility. You could think that it is your duty to fix the other person's issues, but you may end up giving and giving to partners who are undeserving of your time. Once you've learned how to embrace your own emotions and sensitive side, you will stop searching for a partner to give this to you. A good relationship is one where you're able to bond with your partner on a deeper, spiritual level, rather than having a partner who continually sucks your energy.

LIBRA RISING » ARIES DESCENDANT

As a Libra rising, you are a people person. You enjoy having close relationships with people, and you may have a large number of friends that you meet up with on a regular basis. You're also very attentive to the needs of others, and you know how to compromise and keep the peace in your relationships. Additionally, you present yourself as someone who has good style and an interest in the arts and other cultures. You also place importance on having good manners and being polite to everyone that you meet. However, you may sometimes find it hard to assert yourself and ask for what you want, as you don't want to upset anyone. With an Aries descendant, you probably attract partners who are comfortable taking charge and making the big decisions for you. The people you date probably have big personalities and a confident, go-getter approach to life. However, they may also be overly bossy and sometimes aggressive toward you or fiery and quick to get upset. Your partner may often challenge you and test your patience. It is through your relationships that you are learning how to better stand up for yourself, though. Rather than letting the other person tell you what to do, you have to learn how to take charge of your own life and look less to other people for direction.

SCORPIO RISING » TAURUS DESCENDANT

As a Scorpio rising, you keep your cards close to your chest. You like your privacy and space, and you may not open up that quickly to people. Instead, you prefer to observe from afar to get an idea of who someone really is. You're always digging beneath the surface, wanting to understand how people work, and you never take anyone or anything at face value. However, you may struggle with controlling tendencies and might only want people to see a certain side of you. With a Taurus descendant, you're probably drawn to partners who are less complex and who have a calm, gentle nature. What you see is what you get with them, which you appreciate, as you tend to keep so many of your own desires and emotions hidden. You may look to your romantic partners to provide stability and security for you, but you could end up attracting people who are super stubborn and set in their ways or who end up indulging too much in material comforts. Once you realize that you are capable of facing those shadow sides of yourself and achieving greater emotional stability, you won't feel like you need a partner to provide this for you. It is also through your relationships that you are learning how to be less controlling and more willing to share your innermost feelings, as well as your resources, with another person.

SAGITTARIUS RISING » GEMINI DESCENDANT

As a Sagittarius rising, you look at life with a glass-half-full mentality. You have an optimistic attitude, and you are curious to learn about different cultures, opinions, and belief systems. Having the freedom to travel and explore the world is important to you, and you may also enjoy reading, researching, and educating yourself on new subjects of interest. However, sometimes you may be overly enthusiastic, promising more than you can deliver or being very loud about your own opinions without considering what someone else may think. With a Gemini descendant, you're probably drawn to partners who are a bit more tactful and can gracefully navigate social situations. They have the wittiness and poise that you feel you may lack. However, you could often end up with people who are prone to changing their minds often and who can't make up their feelings about you. The people you date may turn out to be flaky and unreliable, which is frustrating for you since you are so big on honesty and are upfront about your feelings. The idea of having your personal freedom compromised is what may scare you the most about being in a relationship, so you may subconsciously attract people who aren't ready for commitment. When you become more flexible with your plans for the future, as well as staying open-minded in conversations that may challenge your specific set of beliefs, you will be able to have a relationship where you can have in-depth conversations and connect on a deeper level.

CAPRICORN RISING » CANCER DESCENDANT

As a Capricorn rising, you are ambitious, and you may strive to be well known and respected in your specific field. However, you also put a lot of pressure on yourself to achieve your goals, and it may feel like there's always another milestone that you have to reach.

It may be difficult for you to stand still and be satisfied with your accomplishments. In your interactions with people, you may come across as reserved, and it can be difficult for others to tell what you're really feeling. You never want to appear weak or vulnerable. With a Cancer descendant, you may attract partners who have a warm, maternal energy. You may look to the people you date to nurture you and offer emotional guidance and comfort. At the same time, you might end up with partners who are moody, and you can never predict how they may feel on a given day. It may also feel like they smother you with affection and want to attend to your every need. Through relationships, you are learning that it's okay to share your feelings and vulnerabilities with people, as that is how you build greater intimacy in relationships. Once you learn how not to be so self-critical and develop greater compassion for yourself, you won't rely on a partner to fill your needs for you in such an extreme way.

AQUARIUS RISING » LEO DESCENDANT

As an Aquarius rising, you are a true visionary. Your mind is usually far in the future, and you're always coming up with ways you can change the world and make a real impact on society. You're vocal about the causes you care about, but you may struggle with showing affection in your relationships. You may hold people at arm's length, and you could have a fear of people threatening your independence or trying to control you. You also probably stand out as being different, and you may think of yourself as an outsider who is a bit detached and floats between social circles. With Leo descendant, you tend to attract partners who pour their whole heart into the people and work that they care about. They may have a lot of passion and creativity, and you admire how they're able to wear their heart on their sleeves and be vocal about their feelings. However, you may also end up with partners who are overly dramatic and self-centered. They may go out of their way to stir the pot to get a reaction out of you or only think of themselves when making decisions. Through your relationships, you are learning how to experiment with creativity and prioritize your own inner child, rather than feeling like you have to always put community or society at large first. Once you learn that it's okay to care about things that may seem a bit self-indulgent, and get over feeling uncomfortable with sharing your emotions, you will stop attracting partners who completely steal the spotlight and demand all of your attention.

PISCES RISING » VIRGO DESCENDANT

As a Pisces rising, you are highly sensitive and intuitive. You have the ability to pick up on how other people are feeling as well as the energy around you, but sometimes it may be hard to separate your emotions from those of someone else. You could need frequent time alone to recharge and tend to your creative hobbies. Because it's so easy for you to empathize with others, you are very giving, and you may go out of your way to help people out. However, you run the risk of losing your sense of self along the way, and it may be difficult to pinpoint what your true desires really are. With a Virgo descendant, you're drawn to people who are responsible and put together and don't get overwhelmed by everyday details. You may look to your partners to organize your life for you or solve all of your problems, and they could help you feel level-headed and grounded. On the flip side of that, though, you may end up with people who are critical of you and make you feel like you're not competent enough to do these things on your own. They can also be nitpicky or overly negative. Through your relationships, you are learning how to be more discerning of who and what you give your energy to. When you become comfortable taking charge of your own destiny and finding greater structure for yourself, you will stop attracting people who are overbearing and try to control your every move.

Going Deeper Together: The Eighth House

THE EIGHTH HOUSE builds upon the themes brought up in the seventh house and takes them one step further. Whereas the seventh is about establishing commitment and building partnerships, the eighth has to do with more intimate matters like sharing finances, dealing with loss, overcoming relationship issues, and having difficult conversations with your partner. I want to linger on the money aspect of this house first. The eighth house encompasses finances you may share or receive from someone else, so this might include inheritance, investments, a loan, or a big bonus at work. In the realm of relationships, though, it applies to how you manage your finances with your partner, like whether or not you have a joint bank account or how much you rely on the other person to financially support you. Planets placed in the eighth and the sign ruling the eighth in your chart will show how you manage money with someone else. Jupiter or Venus in the eighth often indicate receiving financial benefits through a partner, while Mars in the eighth may mean you like to keep your independence there, or you may often run into conflict over shared finances.

Another area that the eighth house covers is understanding human behavior and bringing up topics and feelings that are normally kept repressed or considered taboo. An emphasis on the eighth house in your chart, with one or more planets residing there, indicates that you may enjoy deep conversations with other people and uncovering what really makes them tick. There may be a natural interest in psychology or talking about other people's trauma and personal problems. Oftentimes, you may realize where you can improve upon your own patterns and behaviors because of a relationship issue that you are faced with. Relationships act as a catalyst for your own personal growth. In addition, loss and death fall under the umbrella of the eighth house, so this can either refer to a break-up or experiencing the literal death of someone you know. If you have one or more planets in the eighth, you are probably no stranger to experiencing loss in your life, but you usually come out of these difficult periods feeling like you've shed an old, outdated version of yourself and transformed for the better.

Finally, the eighth house has to do with physical intimacy. We went over how the fifth house is the fun, playful side to sex, where you're doing it to experience pleasure. The sex associated with the eighth is more like a merging of two people, where you're deepening the bond between you—and there's nothing casual about it. In addition, the eighth house includes sexual exploration and how you may go through continual transformation with what you enjoy.

To sum it all up, the sign ruling your eighth house and the planets placed within this house point to how you go about self-improvement and your approach to building greater intimacy with someone. Having Uranus in the eighth or Aquarius ruling this house can mean that you experience this process of loss and rebirth quite suddenly, or you may need an element of space in your close relationships so that you don't feel controlled by someone else. To contrast, having the moon in the eighth or Cancer ruling this house means that you find greater emotional fulfillment through exploring themes related to psychology, death, or helping other people with their problems. You may be familiar with emotional difficulties, and you're able to form a deeper bond with someone by being open about your feelings.

CHAPTER 9

Blending Everything Together

After reading the previous chapter, some of you may have noted that you have your moon, Venus, Mars, or other planets falling in one of those three houses. I myself have the sun, Mercury, and Saturn in my seventh house, and my moon and Venus in the eighth, which is probably why I'm so obsessed with analyzing relationships. However, many people don't have any planets in these houses. If any or all of these houses appear to be "empty" in your chart, that is no indicator of whether or not you will ever have a serious relationship in your life! I cannot tell you how many times I've had people message me thinking that they will be single forever because they have no planets in their seventh house. Planets or no planets, you will want to familiarize yourself with this step-by-step guide on how to interpret these houses, so that you can better understand how they manifest in your life.

To start, choose the fifth, seventh, or eighth house to focus on for this exercise, and go through all of the following steps in relation to it. Then repeat with the next house. You may also want to bookmark Part One of this book, so that you can flip back and forth between the meanings of all the planets and signs as you apply them to the houses.

1. **CHECK TO SEE WHAT PLANETS (IF ANY) ARE LOCATED IN A PARTICULAR HOUSE.**

If you don't have planets in the specific house that you are looking at, like the eighth house, for example, you can immediately move on to step two. If you do have planets there, the energy of that planet will come through in the themes pertaining to that house. The house symbolizes the area of life where the planet can carry out its actions, so you will want to blend the meaning of the planet with the signification of the house. For instance, let's say you have the moon in your eighth house, as seen in the diagram on the next page. We learned that the moon symbolizes your innermost emotions, how you express your feelings, and how you nurture yourself. Therefore, its house placement in your chart will indicate what area of life your emotions are strongly tied to, as well as what activity you get the most emotional fulfillment from. The eighth house symbolizes the more intimate side to relationships, like sharing money and resources or opening up and discussing more emotionally charged topics. It's also a house that pertains to loss and rebirth, as well as deep inner healing. We can then deduce that having the moon in the eighth house of your chart means that you may feel the most secure when having intimate conversations with people, and you could get the most emotional fulfillment through studying topics like psychology, the occult, or going to therapy yourself. It could be that your relationships help you to understand what emotional patterns and behaviors you can transform for the better.

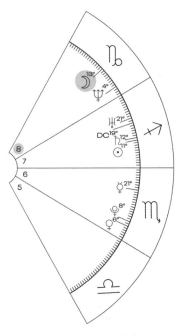

The moon in the eighth house.

2. LOCATE THE SIGN THAT RULES THE HOUSE

No matter whether you have planets in a house or not, you will always want to locate what sign is ruling that house. This will be the sign that is placed on the outer border of the house when you're looking at your birth chart, seen in the diagram on page 118. Remember, with whole sign houses, one sign = one house. The sign ruling a specific house influences how you express those house themes in your life. We got into this a little when looking at the seventh house and descendant line interpretations, but you can apply the same approach to the fifth and eighth houses as well. For this step, you're taking the qualities of the sign and blending it with the meaning of the house.

Referring back to the same chart, you will notice that Libra is ruling the fifth house. This may mean that you are attracted to people who have a strong aesthetic and who value art and culture (Libra). You may also enjoy collaborating (Libra) on creative projects (fifth house), and it could be that a partner (Libra) inspires you to fully express yourself and tap into what makes you unique (fifth house). The one-on-one conversations you have with others (Libra) are important in your journey toward developing greater self-confidence (fifth house). Now, look at the seventh house of the chart, noting how Sagittarius rules this house. In addition to the fifth house themes, you might also be drawn to someone who is from a different cultural background (Sagittarius). The people you date or end up in a relationship with (seventh house) may also have a love for learning, or they could urge you to think optimistically or become more spiritually minded (Sagittarius). They may even open you up to looking at the world differently (Sagittarius).

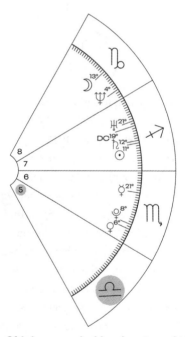

The fifth house ruled by the sign of Libra.

3. **COMBINE ALL OF THE ABOVE**

Taking what you've learned over the past few chapters about planets, signs, and houses, you are now going to blend all of these elements to get the most accurate read on that specific house. The signification of the house + planets placed inside + sign ruling that house = how you approach that side of dating and relationships.

Let's continue using our previous example, again highlighted in the diagram below. In the chart, you can see that the sun, Saturn, and Uranus are all placed in Sagittarius in the seventh house. Having two or more planets in one house can feel a bit overwhelming, so let's break it down one at a time. We already went over what it means to have Sagittarius ruling the seventh house. With the sun in the seventh house, though, you may look to relationships to give you a clearer sense of who you are, and your close interactions with people urge you to see your full potential. In addition, you may find that in all parts of your life, you accomplish a lot more with the help of a partner.

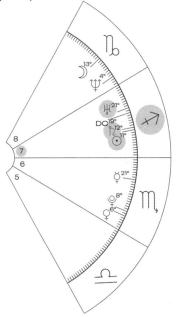

The sun, Saturn, and Uranus all located in Sagittarius, seventh house.

However, also having Saturn in the seventh house may complicate relationships a bit. With Saturn there, you may lack confidence when dating, or you could have a fear of being your full, authentic self around new romantic prospects. You take relationship commitment very seriously, and you need to be able to see long-term potential with whomever you date. It's also likely that relationships will get easier as you get older. Finally, if we add Uranus into the mix, it might be that you still like a bit of unpredictability in your relationships, or you may desire periodic space from your partner to go off and do your own thing. Even in your closest relationships, you still like to maintain your sense of independence. If you're not owning your need for freedom, though, it might be that you attract partners who are a bit chaotic or unsure of their feelings for you.

You can see that the qualities of Sagittarius, the sun, Saturn, and Uranus all play a role in how this person probably approaches relationships. As we just saw in this chart example, there will often be contradictions between planets placed in the same parts of your chart, as in the case of Saturn and Uranus, or you may find that a planet and a sign have seemingly opposite meanings, as with the planet Saturn and the sign Sagittarius. This doesn't mean that one planet or sign is more relevant than the other, and you may find that you experience traits from each. Humans are complicated beings, and astrology is simply reflecting that.

BONUS POINT: Locate the ruling planet of the sign ruling a house and the aspects it is making to other planets in your chart.

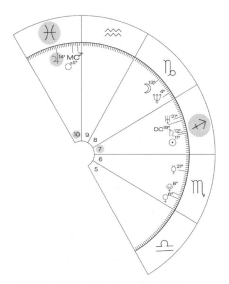

Sagittarius rules the seventh house.
Its ruler, Jupiter, is in Pisces in the tenth house.

Once you've mastered the above steps, you can take this exercise a little further, if you would like. You may have started to observe that some of the planets share similar characteristics with the signs. The moon is associated with the home, just like Cancer, while Mars has a very action-oriented energy that is similar to Aries. This is because each planet corresponds with, or "rules," a specific sign.

I use the traditional rulerships for the twelve signs, so Neptune, Uranus, and Pluto are excluded from the below. Memorizing the signs and their planetary rulers is key, especially when you are interpreting the houses and angles of your chart (in this case, the descendant line and the fifth, seventh, and eighth houses). If you don't have any planets in a particular house, and you want to look at either your descendant or the fifth, seventh, and eighth houses of your chart, then you can gather more information by locating the planet that rules that angle and house. To do so, identify the sign on the border of that house or the sign in which your descendant falls, and then check below to see what the ruler of that sign is. Next, locate where that planet is placed in your chart.

ARIES → MARS

TAURUS → VENUS

GEMINI → MERCURY

CANCER → THE MOON

LEO → THE SUN

VIRGO → MERCURY

LIBRA → VENUS

SCORPIO → MARS

SAGITTARIUS → JUPITER

CAPRICORN → SATURN

AQUARIUS → SATURN

PISCES → JUPITER

Knowing the ruling planets and where they fall in your chart will add an additional layer of interpretation to a house for you. Referring back to the diagram on page 121, you can see that Sagittarius rules the seventh house and descendant. So, you would then locate where Jupiter (the planet that rules Sagittarius) falls in your chart. Jupiter's placement, by sign and by house, would then tell you more about what you may be looking for in a partner, how and where your relationships might start out, as well as what you deem to be important in a relationship.

Following on from this, let's say Jupiter falls in Pisces in the tenth house of your chart. That would indicate that you may also be attracted to people who are driven to succeed and have a prominent career, or that you could end up working with your partner at some point or meeting someone through your job. In addition, you might look for someone who is also creative, sensitive, or who is very in tune with their own emotions or spirituality. Both the tenth house and Pisces themes will find their way back into your relationships.

I know this is a lot of technical information to take in, so well done on getting this far. Now that we're almost at the end of understanding your birth chart through the lens of relationships, I hope you've been able to identify parts that resonate with you, as well as put a finger on areas you may want to improve upon. You can return to your birth chart time and time again, continually discovering something new about yourself and, through these discoveries, gaining greater confidence in who you are as an individual.

CHAPTER 10

But What if Relationships Don't Work for Me?

So, you've now got a full handle on your birth chart and what it means for your relationships, but now what? This chapter is specifically for anyone who feels like they just *can't* catch a break in their love life. It may seem like you're always the single friend, or you could be stuck in a cycle of dating the same type of person over and over again. In astrology, there are certain chart placements that are a little trickier to navigate than others, so I have grouped together those that tend to cause some difficulty with love and dating.

First, I want to make it clear that none of these placements mean that you are doomed in love! That's not the way I look at astrology, and you shouldn't either. There is a tendency when people first start learning astrology to fixate on the so-called "negative" parts of their chart. Instead of saying that you hate having your moon in Scorpio, or that you're doomed because you have Saturn in the seventh house, I want you to realize through reading this that those relationship challenges are actually your greatest gift. Though you may have a few more hurdles to overcome in the realm of relationships than other people, this is the part of your life where you're gaining the most wisdom and a better understanding of yourself.

So far in this book, we've gone over signs, planets, aspects, and houses, and we've learned all of the technical information behind them. For each category in this chapter, I've put placements together that share a common thread, so that you can see how they play out in your love life. I would not freak out if you have multiple of the below placements in your chart. All of the five categories listed beneath apply to me—which is the main reason I'm so fascinated by relationship astrology. As I've mentioned before, my love life was horrendous throughout my teens and twenties, but relationship challenges are the area that I'm determined to become more self-aware of and learn the most about.

ALWAYS THE SINGLE FRIEND

- Saturn in the seventh house
- Venus–Saturn or moon–Saturn aspects
- Venus or moon in Capricorn
- Capricorn ruling your seventh house
- The ruler of your seventh house in a conjunction, square, or opposition to Saturn

If you have any of the above Saturnian placements in your chart, you may sometimes wonder why you don't have as many relationships or flings as some of your friends do. You could watch everyone around you couple up while wondering why you're always the single one. With Saturn or Saturn-ruled signs influencing your love life, you may have an intense fear of rejection, which causes you to put your guard up when dating. You might take a super serious approach to relationships, and it could be challenging for you to relax and just go with the flow when you're getting to know someone. You need to be sure of where you stand with the other person at all times, and you may get anxious when they want to keep things casual or don't set a firm plan for a next date.

You can also be very critical of yourself in relationships, and you may beat yourself up over not sending the right type of text or revealing your emotions for the other person too soon. You may feel like you have to follow a strict dating protocol, such as never reaching out to the other person first or not sleeping with the other person until a certain number of dates have gone by. Saturn loves rules and structure, but unfortunately there are no real rules when it comes to love. By worrying so much about if you're following the correct relationship steps, you may keep the other person from getting to know the real, authentic version of yourself. Additionally, you may have a scarcity mindset with dating, thinking that if it doesn't work out with one specific person, then no one will ever want to be with you again. You could have a fear of taking relationship risks and putting your feelings out there, because you don't want to scare anyone off by doing the wrong thing. Rather than trying to guess what the other person may do, you have to realize that you have the power to decide who you do and don't like. Over time, you're discovering your own inner authority in relationships.

It could also feel like you're always going after the wrong types of people. You may complain when the person you are dating turns out not to be so great or completely different from who you thought they were. Your first instinct might be to blame them or wonder things like, *Why does this always happen to me?* What you may not realize, though, is that you are going after people who you know won't work out in the long-term. You may not even realize that you are doing this, but there is usually a deep inner fear of fully letting your guard down and relying on someone. Subconsciously, you would rather pick a person who you know won't turn into anything serious, or people who are emotionally unavailable, because you want to protect your feelings.

In addition, Saturn causes feelings of separation, so at times you may feel lonely, not only in your love life but also with friendships. You may have the outlook that other people are better than you or more deserving of love and attention. It might be that you were shy in school growing up, and those feelings of self-consciousness still carry over into your adult life when you're meeting new people. The irony is that your own thoughts are often the only thing that is holding you back from forming connections.

If none of the above has resonated with you so far, these placements can sometimes indicate getting into one relationship early on and staying in that relationship forever. For example, you might be someone who is still in your twenties, but you have already been in a relationship for seven or eight years. You take your commitments very seriously, so you are willing to stay in a relationship and not walk away at the first sign of difficulty.

No matter how you may experience these placements in your chart, it's important to know that they do get easier over time. Your love life may become a prominent focus during your Saturn Return (see page 176), around the ages of 27–30. That might be an important period for you, where you overcome your relationship fears and develop greater confidence with dating. You may finally feel more comfortable in your own skin, or you could just get fed up with all of your fearful mindsets that hold you back. Though relationships are where you encounter some of the most challenging life lessons, they are also the part of your life that you are here to master and gain wisdom on.

STRUGGLING TO BE IN CONTROL

- Pluto in the seventh house
- Venus–Pluto or moon–Pluto aspects
- Venus or moon in Scorpio
- Venus or the moon in the eighth house
- Scorpio ruling your seventh house
- The ruling planet of your seventh house in a conjunction, square, or opposition to Pluto

If you have any of the above placements in your chart, you are pretty black and white about who you do and don't like. You are either not interested in someone at all or head over heels for one specific person. You're very intuitive, so you may be able to sense immediately if someone is meant to be in your life. The attraction needs to be there right off the bat, so you're not really someone who is willing to stick around and see if the chemistry eventually develops. Though your friends might criticize you for being too picky, you would rather be single for longer periods of time than settle for someone you feel lukewarm about. Dating apps might be particularly difficult for you, because it's hard to get a good read on someone. With online dating, there usually isn't that same intensity you may experience when you're encountering a person in real life for the first time.

Once you decide that you like someone, it might be challenging for you to keep the relationship light and casual. You want to bond with whomever you're dating on a deeper level and get to the bottom of who that person really is. You may struggle with making small talk on a first date or texting about random things that went on that day. Instead, you probably prefer talking about topics that go super in-depth, like a person's family relationships, their past heartbreaks, or what they are passionate about. You like to develop this intimacy with another person very early on in your relationships.

One trait you may want to be wary of, though, is your tendency to get obsessive over love interests. With Scorpio and Pluto influencing your love life, you may enjoy dissecting other people's lives, but talking about your own emotions might not be your strongest suit. Your romantic feelings for people are often very intense, but you keep them buried. You may go for years harboring a crush on someone, while the other person has no idea that you even like them, or you could get fixated on needing a certain outcome. It could be hard for you to let go and move on when you find out that someone isn't interested, or if a relationship has suddenly ended without you being the one to end it. The more someone pulls away, the harder you may try to get them to stay. On the other hand, if a partner or good friend betrays your trust in any way or you're just over them, you are swiftly able to cut that person out of your life.

Additionally, you have strong sleuthing skills, so you may constantly be checking your crush's social media or digging up information on a person's ex from five years ago. You enjoy carefully gathering information on the people that you like, but there is such a thing as knowing too much. You may end up spiraling and getting paranoid about whether your partner is talking to someone else. Jealousy might come up frequently when dating, as you want the other person to like you, and only you. Aware of how strong your own emotions can be, you may just immediately assume that the other person is hiding their feelings and keeping secrets as well. This mindset can make it hard for you to fully trust the people you date. However, it is only by opening up and communicating these fears that you are able to form a stronger bond with your partner.

A final way these placements may manifest is in choosing to like people who you know are already taken or just aren't emotionally available. Even if you are aware that the person you like isn't necessarily right for you, you will still find ways to hold their attention. You may crave the power and validation that comes from knowing that you are wanted. These behaviors may stem from an insecurity, like not feeling worthy of being loved, so you're drawn to relationships where it's a challenge to get the other person. When you work on developing greater self-esteem, you won't end up in such drama-filled situationships, and going after people who don't reciprocate your feelings will no longer be of interest to you.

The main takeaway to know with Scorpio, Pluto, or eighth house placements is that relationships will be the biggest point of transformation for you throughout your life. Every single romantic encounter may make you more aware of certain habits and mindsets that you need to release, and any heartbreak that you go through will push you to discover hidden skills you never knew you had. Though they are extremely difficult in the moment, these relationship challenges are helping you to come into a new and improved version of yourself.

CONSTANTLY FALLING FOR THE WRONG PEOPLE

- Neptune in the seventh house
- Venus–Neptune or moon–Neptune aspects
- Venus or moon in Pisces
- Pisces ruling your seventh house
- The ruling planet of your seventh house in a conjunction, square, or opposition to Neptune

If you have any of the above placements in your chart, you may always be searching for a fairy-tale romance. However, this endless quest for the perfect relationship may often leave you disappointed when reality doesn't match your high expectations. It can be hard for you to identify red flags when dating, and it's like all of your common sense goes out the door when you like someone. After one date, you might be thinking of your future wedding with a person, or imagining what it will be like when they meet your friends and parents for the first time. You get sucked into planning a future with someone you barely know. Rather than stopping to consider if you even like them, you may often get hung up on the serendipitous way in which you met or that one cute line they said on your first date.

You may have these seemingly amazing stories of how you met someone, like, "I was waiting for the train, and this guy I made eye contact with asked for my number," or, "I've reconnected with my childhood crush from when I was 14." The more your love life resembles a romantic comedy, the better. Meanwhile, the reality of the situation may be that the other person has gone days without responding to your last text or is constantly rescheduling on you and not being respectful of your time. You may brush over these minor details, preferring to live inside the fantasy you have created. You have to learn how to take the people you date at face value. When someone shows you who they really are, you need to listen.

Additionally, you may have a pattern of getting into relationships with people who take and take from you. You often go after those who you think you can save, and you could end up with partners who are lost in life, who struggle with addiction, or who just aren't clear on their emotions for you. It might even be that you take on the other person's issues and make them your own. You may think that if you are extra patient and just try hard enough with a person, then the relationship will work out perfectly. You have a lot of empathy for other people, but again, you may be too focused on the potential of who someone could be, rather than facing the reality of the relationship and who they are. Your innate compassion and loving nature can often lead you to give all of your energy away to people who don't deserve it. However, doing this only leads to frustration and inner resentment when you realize that the other person isn't putting in the same effort.

Another behavior that I see happen frequently with these placements is that you may lose yourself in your partner's hobbies and interests, completely forgetting what activities you enjoy doing for yourself. Usually there is something lacking in your own life that needs your attention, which you are distracting yourself from by handling someone else's problems.

Finally, it's important for you to recognize that the honeymoon phase of a relationship will not last forever. Once you've been in a relationship for a while, you may start to get turned off by those everyday, mundane parts of being with someone. In your romantic fantasies, you probably weren't envisioning that you would have to clean up after your partner or talk about who will pay the bills or run errands. You may need to find little ways to keep the romance alive in your relationship, like planning a weekly date night or surprising your partner with a thoughtful gift every now and then.

All of the above isn't to say that true love is not possible for you. But if you want a partner who does things like bring you flowers or go out of their way to plan romantic dates, you will only find it when you learn how to prioritize yourself and stand your ground on what you want out of a relationship. With Pisces and Neptune influencing your love life, healthier relationships typically come when you learn how to set boundaries for yourself. You might want to find a creative hobby, spiritual practice, or act of community service that gives you that feeling of helping people or having a deeper purpose in life. You are at your best when you're channeling your emotional energy into an activity that supports you and lights you up, rather than giving so much of yourself away to other people.

NEEDING PERIODIC SPACE

- Uranus in the seventh house
- Venus–Uranus or moon–Uranus aspects
- Venus or moon in Aquarius
- Aquarius ruling your seventh house
- The ruler of your seventh house in a conjunction, square, or opposition to Uranus

If you have any of the above placements in your birth chart, having independence and space to live life on your own terms is extremely important to you. Though you may think you want a committed, long-term relationship, there's another side of you that starts to feel smothered when you fall into a regular routine with a partner, and you could grow restless when the relationship starts to feel too calm and settled. Once you get the affection you crave, there may be a part of you that rejects it. You could fear that your freedom will be compromised if you fully commit to sharing your life with someone, so you may end up going after people who don't have the potential to last in the long term or who give you too much space by being on and off about their feelings.

From a young age, you may have always felt like you've stood out in some way. Even if you have a lot of friends, there may be a part of you that feels like you don't completely fit in. In your friendships, you might float between several different groups, never wanting to be tied down to just one circle of people. With romantic relationships, you could hold your partner at arm's length or struggle to fully commit, and you may sometimes get criticized for coming across as detached or unemotional. It mainly appears this way to other people because you can get so "in your own head," overanalyzing a situation or wondering what the future might look like with a person.

You may be drawn to relationships that are long-distance, non-monogamous, or that go against the status quo. You could enjoy rebelling against the standard dating protocol, and you may not see the point in getting married or going through the typical motions of dating. When it comes to what other people consider to be the norm for relationships, you always stop and question whether it is the right path for you. Additionally, you might often be attracted to people who are quirky in some way and who stand out for being unique. The weirder a person is, the more you're into them. Though you can sometimes end up with people who live chaotic lifestyles, on the upside you always approach dating with an open mind. You won't brush anyone off just because they aren't "your usual type."

One area where you might struggle the most in relationships is showing your partner that you like them. That may seem silly to some people, but you might feel uncomfortable discussing your romantic feelings and explicitly telling someone that you care about them. Physical affection might not be a big priority for you, either. You're better at analyzing situations and coming up with solutions for the future, so it could be difficult for you to be in the present moment with someone. These behaviors don't mean you don't care; you simply show your love for people through having in-depth conversations or encouraging them to chase after far-fetched hopes and dreams. However, the struggle to emotionally open up may mean that you end up attracting people who aren't so sure about you. It may also be that your relationships get super intense very quickly but then end abruptly, out of nowhere, after only a short period of time. You may blame the other person for being non-committal or undecided on what they want out of a relationship, when really, they're just picking up on your energy and reflecting it back to you.

Because you are so used to living life on your own terms, it may also be hard adjusting to consulting with a romantic partner before you make big decisions. You want to know that you have the option to act on a whim: for example, being able to pick up and move to another city if you want to one day. You don't like feeling like your decisions are being controlled by someone else. Part of having a successful relationship, though, is knowing when to compromise and not always putting yourself first. Through your relationships, you are learning how to achieve a balance between being able to go off and do your own thing from time to time, while still showing up for the other person and carrying out your relationship duties. Decisions don't always need to be your way or the highway.

As you date and gain greater relationship experience, you may come to realize that you need to accept your inner weirdness rather than searching for it in other people. You have all of these original ideas and desires to live your life differently from everyone else, but you have to become more comfortable with the ways in which you stand out. You may come to realize that you don't need a partner to fill this void for you.

INTENSE RELATIONSHIP ANXIETY

- Chiron in the fifth or seventh house
- Chiron close to the ascendant
- Venus–Chiron or moon–Chiron aspects
- The ruler of your seventh house in aspect to Chiron
- Chiron in Libra

We haven't yet talked much about the planetoid Chiron, but I wanted to bring it up in the context of difficult relationship placements, because understanding Chiron is the key to healing deep-seated relationship wounds. Wherever Chiron is placed in your birth chart shows an area of life where you may struggle with never feeling good enough. If you have Chiron configured in any of the above placements, you experience that feeling of lack and anxiety in your love life. Relationships may bring up a lot of heavy emotions or memories of past trauma. There may have been traumatic experiences when you were younger, like bullying, or you may have gone through a difficult dating or sexual experience that now makes it hard for you to develop intimacy with people as an adult. For instance, I often see Chiron placed in the seventh house when someone's parents got divorced early on in their life, or if from a young age they viewed their parents' relationship or relationships in general as being stressful. There is a lot of hesitancy to date and enter into a partnership with someone, because you don't want to experience that same pain.

With Chiron influencing your love life, you may struggle with feelings of self-worth in your relationships, believing that you simply aren't lovable enough. In the case of having Chiron in the first house, close to the ascendant line, you could even feel like you're physically unattractive and not hot enough to date certain people. Of course, all of these thoughts are in your own head—none of it is actually true. Because you feel that way about yourself, though, you carry that low self-worth energy into your relationships. If you don't believe in yourself, then you're not going to attract partners who do, either.

Coping mechanisms for Chiron often involve overcompensating in that area of life. Going back to the Chiron in the first house example, you may fixate on your appearance and feel like you need to buy the most expensive clothing or fix some aspect of your body in order to feel worthy. If you have Venus or the moon in aspect to Chiron or Chiron in the seventh house, you may be drawn to people who are wounded or need fixing. You might always root for the underdog and give your energy away to people who need your help. However, you could end up in a pattern where you're always doing more for your romantic partners or friends, but they aren't giving you that same effort and consideration in return. No matter how hard you try to fix someone else's problems, it's never enough, and you may have this constant feeling that something is missing in your relationships.

In order to heal Chiron, you have to become comfortable being vocal about your experiences and finding people who have gone through something similar. By sharing your hardships with other people, you will in turn heal yourself. Ironically, having Chiron in this part of your chart can make you a relationship expert. Being vulnerable with others about your anxieties is cathartic, and it often offers you perspective on how to transform your Chiron wound. You just have to make sure that you're actually applying the same advice that you're giving out to others to yourself.

A synastry chart. The partner's chart on the
outside has been shaded here to make it easier
to see how the two charts work together.

PART THREE

Are We Compatible?
Your Synastry Chart

Before we get into this section, I want you to first forget everything you know about sun sign compatibility. You may think that you have an idea of what signs work with yours and what signs don't, but as we've learned repeatedly throughout this book, astrology goes way beyond your sun sign. You might often hear misconceptions like if you are a Virgo, then you can't be with an Aquarius, or if you are an Aries, you should only date people who are Leo or Sagittarius. Compatibility is not that black and white, though, and astrology is ultimately unable to tell if a relationship will or won't work with another person. It simply describes where a couple's strengths and challenges lie within that relationship.

Synastry is the term used to define the practice of comparing your birth chart to someone else's. It shows how the planets, signs, and houses of one person's chart interact with those of another person's chart. Synastry can show why two people may have challenges in having open communication, or why they may experience trust issues. It can also indicate the more positive sides to a relationship, too, like why you feel at home in another person's presence, or how you both make great travel companions or laugh at each other's jokes. In some cases, synastry can even indicate the circumstances under which two people met. Did the romantic relationship start off as being friends first or did the couple meet through work? I will be showing you how to delineate all of these different elements throughout this section. What synastry *cannot* do, though, is explicitly say that a person is or isn't right for you. So, no more using astrology to write someone off before you even get to know them! Romantic relationships aside, you can try looking at your synastry with a family member or a close friend. Chances are, a lot of what I'm about to discuss will apply to them, too. I also want to add that you don't need to go looking for someone who is "compatible" with you, because you naturally attract people who have charts that align with yours.

As you read Part Three, try not to fixate on the challenging aspects you may have with a partner. All relationships have their fair share of both easy and difficult synastry alignments. Instead, I want you to step back and look at the overall connections between the two charts, identifying what comes naturally between you and your partner, as well as what areas may need more focus or improvement. One major thing I also want to stress is that you should never use synastry to justify someone's behavior in a relationship. You may share so many great chart match-ups, but if the other person is acting hot and cold in their feelings toward you or isn't respecting your time or treating you well, then they most likely aren't the best partner for you.

How to get started with synastry

1. **PULL UP YOUR SYNASTRY CHART.** To pull up a synastry chart, you will again want to use a website like astro.com or astro-seek.com. After you've entered in your birth information, there is an option on both of these websites to select "Synastry" from the chart type option, which is located in the "Chart type" drop-down list on astro.com, or on the right sidebar if you already have your birth chart pulled up on astro-seek.com. From there, you will be able to enter in a second person's birth information.

2. **TRAIN YOUR EYE.** Familiarize yourself with the synastry chart, like the one pictured at the start of Part Three. Your birth chart should be the one in the center wheel, while the other person's chart is placed on the outer wheel around yours.

3. **TAKE NOTE OF MATCHUPS BETWEEN THE TWO CHARTS.** When you are looking at the diagram at the start of this chapter, you may notice how some of the planets in one person's chart fall close to the planets and the angles in another person's chart. I've used my birth chart on the inside, with my partner's chart on the outside. At first glance, you might see how we both have Mars in Cancer, touching each other. You can also look at the Taurus section of the chart and see that my partner's sun in Taurus falls next to my Midheaven (MC) in Taurus. We'll go through how you can notice these types of alignments when you are doing your own synastry chart. Additionally, you can see that my partner's planets in the outer ring fall into specific houses of my chart in the inner ring. For instance, his Mercury in Aries falls into the ninth house of my chart, while his Venus in Gemini activates my eleventh house.

4. **FLIP THE CHARTS.** To read these overlays the other way around, experiment with flipping the two charts so that the other person's chart is placed on the inside instead. To do this, you would enter your partner's birth information for the main birth data entry before adding your own birth information as the partner's chart. You may notice even more alignments between the two charts by looking at it from this different perspective.

It may take some time to get used to interpreting a synastry chart, and every time you return to one you will probably notice something new. Synastry can be very complex, so to make it easier to understand I have broken it down into four distinct categories we'll take into consideration when doing a chart comparison:

- Sign similarities—what you have in common
- Planetary alignments—complex dynamics
- Angle match-ups—aligned on the bigger picture
- House overlays—shared interests

We won't go into every single planet or sign combination you can have with someone, because I want you to focus on the bigger picture of the two charts interacting. Okay, enough background information, let's get started!

CHAPTER 11

What You Have in Common: Sign Similarities

When you are comparing your chart to someone else's, you will first want to look out for sign similarities. As we've learned, this doesn't just mean your sun sign. For this exercise, you will want to look at the signs of *all* of the planets in both your chart and the other person's, putting a greater emphasis on the luminaries (the sun and moon) and inner planets (Mercury, Venus, and Mars). If you are a bit overwhelmed, a good entry point for seeing if you have sign matchups with someone can be to see what their big three are: their sun, moon, and rising (ascendant). Often, a lot of the people in your life may have a similar big three combination to your own. For example, if you know that you are a Sagittarius rising, then you may end up dating people who have Sagittarius as their sun or moon sign. If your sun is in Cancer, maybe you attract people who have a Cancer rising or Cancer moon. As an Aquarius sun, I have dated my fair share of Aquarius moon men, and many of my female friends have this moon sign as well.

SHARING THE SAME SIGNS

When you have planets or angles in the same signs as someone else, it's like you're on the same page. For example, if you both have the **same sun or rising sign (ascendant)**, you are able to understand each other's core interests, and you may have a similar way of approaching life and processing information. Meanwhile if your **moon signs are the same**, you will probably express your emotions similarly, and it may be easy to understand what the other person is feeling. You could also get emotional fulfillment from doing the same type of activities.

Looking at shared signs across the other planets, having the **same Mercury sign** as someone else may mean that you communicate in a similar manner and conversations flow naturally, while having the **same Venus sign** would mean you share similar values or you have the same aesthetic. You might easily agree on how you want to decorate your home or what social and cultural activities you want to get involved in, for instance. Having the **same Mars signs** would indicate that you approach conflict and go after what you want in the same manner, and you might have similar sex drives or be in agreement on what turns both of you on.

SAME SIGNS, DIFFERENT PLANETS

It's also worth noting the signs in which you both have planets, even if the planets there aren't the same. Having a **sun–moon connection**, meaning one person's sun is the same sign as the other person's moon, is especially significant and something I see frequently in the synastry charts of long-term couples. If you have this configuration with someone, you may feel at home in their presence, like it's easy to open up about your emotions and be comfortable around them. You feel very nurtured by the other person. In addition, when someone's **sun or moon is the same sign as your rising sign**, it's like they are able to fully see you. They immediately get you as a person, and in turn you may help them feel more comfortable being their true self.

It may also be that your **Venus is in the same sign as someone's Mars**. For example, if one person has their Venus in Libra, while the other person has their Mars in Libra, this would indicate a strong initial draw to one another. If you are the Venus partner, you may find the Mars partner's assertion of themselves and how they go after what they want to be attractive. By contrast, a **moon–Mars connection** would be another story. Let's say your moon is in Libra and your partner has their Mars in Libra. The meanings of these two planets differ quite a bit, so the moon person may find the Mars person to be at times insensitive or aggressive. They may trigger a strong emotional reaction from you. For synastry matchups like these, you are always taking the signification of one planet and applying it to the meaning of the other planet.

Before you read on, take a look at your synastry chart and see whether you and your partner have planets that fall in any of the same signs.

In addition to sharing the exact same signs with someone, another way to get a sense of your relationship is by considering whether the same sign modality or element is prominent across both of your charts. Noting where you see planets that are both in water signs or fixed signs, for instance, will also help you to see where you and your partner align. You can also think of element and modality matchups as pointing to where you and the other person share a like-minded approach. If you'd like a refresher on the elements and modalities, turn back to page 11.

Signs by Element

AS WE LOOKED at in Chapter 1, the 12 zodiac signs can be categorized into four different elements: fire, earth, water, and air. Take note of where each of your planets fall, and whether you and your partner share signs of the same element, because it shows areas where the relationship flows easily. Check whether you both have an abundance of planets in water signs, or if you're both earth-sign heavy.

For example, if you have one or more planets in Gemini, then you may enjoy the company of people who have planets in Aquarius or Libra. With that shared air-sign quality in your charts, you probably both place importance on socializing and branching out to meet new people, and you may admire the other person's intellect and enjoy your shared ability to carry on a witty conversation. A great configuration to have with a partner is when your moon signs are in the same element. One person's moon might be in Sagittarius, while the other's moon is in Leo. Therefore, they both have fire sign moons, so not only do they express their emotions in a similar way, but they also have a natural understanding of how the other person might be feeling. They might both be very enthusiastic, and find emotional fulfillment in being creative, taking risks, and finding ways to be playful.

A pattern I often see with long-term couples is that they will share the **same element in their rising signs**. This might be a Gemini rising matched with a Libra rising, both air signs, or a Cancer rising with a Pisces rising, both water signs. Having the same exact rising sign as your partner is also common. The rising sign is your approach to life and the way in which you interact with your immediate environment, so you will often be attracted to people who go about that in a similar way. Two water sign risings will both be very intuitive, and their first instinct may be to take care of people and lend their advice and support. By contrast, if you have a fire sign rising like Aries, it might be a bit more challenging to understand where an earth sign rising like Virgo is coming from. You're ready to jump headfirst into new experiences and take immediate action, while a Virgo rising will definitely be more guarded and critical and will need more time to plan.

Additionally, you will want to consider someone's **planets that fall in compatible signs to your own**. Planets in compatible signs are supportive of one another, so fire signs work well with air signs and earth signs will find similarities with water signs. If your sun is in an air sign like Aquarius, then people with planets in Aries, Leo, or Sagittarius will make you feel good about yourself, and you may feel optimistic and energetic in their company. The same goes if you have planets in Cancer, for instance. You may like to surround yourself with people who have earth sign placements in their chart like Taurus, Virgo, or Capricorn.

Signs by Modality

ANOTHER WAY WE know the signs can be categorized is by modality: cardinal, fixed, and mutable signs. Though interactions between planets of the same sign element flow easily, there also isn't a whole lot of tension or a desire to grow. In romantic relationships, you need that energy of both partners pushing one another to continually work on and develop different sides of themselves, so it is actually necessary to have some challenging aspects in a synastry chart. Planets that fall in the same sign modality form squares and oppositions to one another, so they have to work a little harder to understand where the other is coming from.

For example, planets that fall in **fixed signs Taurus, Leo, Scorpio, and Aquarius** are usually drawn to one another. They all embody the fixed sign quality of finishing what you've started and being all in on whatever you're passionate about. Therefore, if you are a fixed sign dating another fixed sign, you will appreciate the intensity they bring to the relationship, and you may both put a lot of effort into making the partnership work. Similarly, **cardinal signs Aries, Cancer, Libra,**

and Capricorn will share the similar attribute of preferring to initiate experiences and may feed off of each other's high energy and want to build something concrete together. Finally, the **mutable signs of Gemini, Virgo, Sagittarius, and Pisces** are able to bond over their willingness to keep an open mind to different ways of thinking and can remain flexible when unexpected events come up in the relationship.

I want to linger on **oppositions**, which are planets that fall in signs exactly opposite to one another, because they are so prevalent in couples' charts. When looking for oppositions, prioritize those between the inner planets in you and your partner's charts, like the sun and the moon or the moon and Venus. Relationships act as a mirror a lot of the time, and that is what planets and signs in opposition to one another indicate. With opposing signs like Cancer and Capricorn or Virgo and Pisces, the other person is reflecting back to you traits you still need to work on integrating into your personality. You and your partner are able to complement one another because you both have qualities that the other person is seeking. With opposing moon signs, for instance, where one person may have a Cancer moon while the other person has a Capricorn moon, the Cancer moon partner may teach the Capricorn moon partner about being more sensitive and less critical, while the Capricorn moon person will show their Cancer moon partner how to be a bit tougher and make their own ambitions more of a priority. They are able to balance each other out.

CHAPTER 12

Complex Dynamics: Planetary Alignments

I want to shift our focus now to seeing whether someone's planets fall exactly on top of your own. It is especially significant if two planets match up exactly at or around the same degree. This is called a conjunction, and it is one of the aspects between planets we covered on page 89. In the diagram below, you'll see where my partner's Saturn falls right on top of my sun and Mercury.

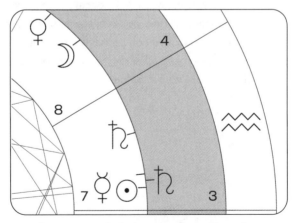

One partner's Saturn conjuncts the other partner's sun and Mercury.

When there are conjunctions like the Saturn–sun one on the opposite page, the outer planet, which is Saturn in this case, will bring a distinct tone to the relationship. Conjunctions between one person's more slow-moving outer planets (like Jupiter, Saturn, Uranus, Neptune, and Pluto) and the other person's luminaries and inner planets (like the sun, moon, Mercury, Venus, and Mars) will result in a specific dynamic between the two people. The associated signification of that outer planet will feature prominently in the relationship.

Take a look at your synastry chart and make a note of any conjunctions that exist between your inner planets and your partner's outer planets, and vice versa. Then use the guide below on outer planet conjunctions to inner planets to help see how a particular dynamic might show up in your relationship.

Once you've familiarized yourself with your conjunctions, you can also start applying everything I will go over next to oppositions, squares, trines, or sextiles between you and your partner's chart as well. It's easier to start with the conjunctions first, though, because these are felt the most intensely and you can spot them right away when looking at two charts.

A MARKER OF LONGEVITY: SATURN CONJUNCTIONS

Aspects between one person's Saturn and another person's inner planets, especially their sun, moon, or Venus, give a relationship longevity. I like to think of Saturn as the glue that binds two people together, so having Saturn aspects in synastry is often a signature of long-term relationships. The two people may understand that the relationship is serious from the start, and they may feel like they have a duty to one another to see things through. The couple will want to put in the effort over time to make the relationship work, and it's unlikely that they will give up on each other when faced with smaller challenges. Saturn aspects can also indicate relationships that stay in your life for some time, where you don't easily forget the other person or keep coming back into contact with them every few years. If someone's Saturn is contacting one of your inner planets, you may look to them for security, and they could seem like the mature one out of the two of you. It may also feel like the Saturn person is teaching you important lessons about yourself, but they may need to watch out for sometimes being overly critical or serious.

A BOOST OF OPTIMISM: JUPITER CONJUNCTIONS

When one person's Jupiter connects with your inner planets, and vice versa, there is humor and silliness in the relationship. The two people may laugh a lot when they're together, and they could also enjoy traveling to new places and encouraging one another to keep an open mind. Jupiter brings warmth to the partnership, so you probably feel very comfortable in each other's presence. Both people in the partnership will also be quite generous, and one person may encourage and motivate the other to develop their talents. There's a distinct positive energy between the two people. If your planets make a connection to someone's Jupiter or your Jupiter to theirs, this is the type of person who you immediately light up around, and you may get really excited to see one another.

OPPORTUNITIES FOR TRANSFORMATION: URANUS, NEPTUNE, PLUTO CONJUNCTIONS

Uranus, Neptune, and Pluto move very slowly through the zodiac, staying in just one sign for over eight years. Therefore, pretty much everyone born within the same generation will have these planets in the same sign. For example, everyone born from about 1988 to 1994 will have Uranus and Neptune in Capricorn, and Pluto in Scorpio.

With Uranus conjunctions, there may be an element of excitement, but also a few unexpected surprises in the relationship. This aspect can indicate a partnership that develops quite quickly, but that can also be a bit off and on. There may also be a feeling of emotional distance between the two people, and it could be challenging to get on the same page about what type of life they want together. Uranus is definitely not the most stable planet, so ideally you would want to have a Saturn aspect between you and your partner's chart to balance out its unpredictability.

Meanwhile, Neptune conjunctions can bring a theme of idealistic romance into the relationship. If someone's Neptune touches your inner planets, you may put them on a pedestal, or you could be blind to their faults. It can be hard to see the other person for who they really are, instead having a vision of who they could be. Additionally, it might be that your partner makes all these big promises that they can't deliver on, or someone in the relationship might end up selflessly giving their energy to the other person. On a more positive note, it's easy for you to intuitively sense how the other is feeling, and it could feel like there's this deeper soul connection between the two of you.

And lastly, Pluto conjunctions bring a strong initial attraction that can sometimes border on obsession. The relationship might feel all-consuming at first, but over time control issues might start to arise. One person in the relationship may have a fear of fully trusting the other, and jealousy could be a problem that comes up as well. On the other hand, Pluto aspects can serve to transform the two people. There might be something about the relationship that changes you for the better, where you learn how to release negative patterns or develop a whole different side of yourself, discovering interests you never knew you had.

WHEN IT FEELS LIKE FATE: NODAL CONJUNCTIONS

The Nodes are not actually planets—they are mathematical points in the sky, but they are worth mentioning in the context of synastry charts. Refer back to page 31 if you need a refresher on the Nodes. Nodal conjunctions happen when one person's inner planet, like their moon or Venus, lands on top of the other person's North or South Node. In general, I try to steer clear of using spiritual woo-woo terms, but when it comes to the Nodes, it is hard to deny that these types of relationships often feel fated, like the two people were always meant to come together at one point or another.

When someone's planet conjuncts your South Node, or the other way around, there is usually an immediate familiarity between the two of you. It may feel like you've known each other forever, even if you've only recently met. You might feel very comfortable in their presence, like you just get each other. However, there may sometimes be the feeling of holding each other back, and the partner whose planets touch your South Node may be wary of you taking bigger risks in your life. However, they may also help you to release negative patterns and any habits that are holding you back from reaching your full potential.

North Node conjunctions definitely aren't as light and fluffy. When someone's planets fall on your North Node, the relationship is pushing you to grow. You are drawn to the other person, but the relationship may feel a bit uncomfortable or scary at first, like something you want to shy away from. The person whose planets are falling on your North Node, though, is urging you to get out of your comfort zone and develop new sides of yourself.

CHAPTER 13

Aligned on What Matters: Angle Matchups

Up until this point, we have mainly gone over the sign matchups and planetary conjunctions you can have with someone, but the angles are just as important to watch out for in a synastry chart. As a reminder, the angles are the ascendant (AC), descendant (DC), Midheaven (MC), and *Imum Coeli* (IC) lines in your chart. On some websites, the DC and the IC aren't labelled, but they will appear as a longer notch mark that falls exactly opposite the AC and MC lines. Revisit page 23 if you need a reminder on angles.

There are two things you will want to note with the angles. First, you will want to identify whether someone's planets fall close to your angles, and vice versa. Next, you will want to see if any of your angles fall in the same signs as the angles of the other person.

Feeling Seen by Your Partner:
When Planets Align with Angles

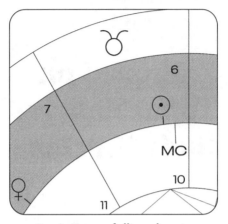

**Sun in Taurus falling close to
the Midheaven (MC) in Taurus.**

THE DIAGRAM ABOVE shows one partner's sun falling on top of the other person's Midheaven (MC). This is the type of alignment you will want to make note of. When someone's planets fall on any of your four angles, they will influence how you express the qualities of that particular angle.

Let's start with the ascendant (AC). If your partner has any of their planets lining up with your AC line, then they will influence how you express yourself, for better or for worse. If someone's Jupiter, Venus, or sun falls on your ascendant, they may encourage you to embody your full self and really engage with the world, as these are positive qualities shared by these planets. You will feel seen and supported by the other person. Meanwhile, having someone's Saturn fall on your AC may prohibit you from being your full self, and you could become more guarded in their presence or feel constantly criticized by them. You may also feel a sense of duty to them. These are all very Saturnian-type themes. Therefore, it's important to take the qualities of the planet touching an angle into consideration as well.

Planet matchups with your Midheaven (MC) often bring themes related to your career and future aspirations into the relationship. If a person's sun or moon falls on your Midheaven, for instance, you may look up to them for their work ethic, they could help to inform your career path, or you could simply be aligned on the same long-term goals as a couple. If someone's planets fall on or close to your descendant (DC), they most likely embody the qualities you subconsciously look for in a good friend or a long-term partner. You may feel comfortable together in one-on-one situations, and it might be easy for you to collaborate and work as a team.

Lastly, when your partner's planets touch your Imum Coeli (IC), especially if it's the sun, moon, Venus, or Jupiter, it is easy to open up emotionally around them, and you may have a desire to start a home and family together. You may even find yourself describing the relationship as feeling "like home" to you. Some planets falling on your IC may be trickier, though. Mars can bring up conflict in the home, and there may be fighting that occurs around what is yours versus what is theirs in your living space, while someone's Saturn on your IC may urge you to get serious about talking through your innermost emotions and discussing any painful memories from childhood. Family members often have IC matchups with one another, so you may want to compare your chart with a parent or a sibling to see if they have planets in the same sign that your IC is in. For example, I have a Scorpio IC in my chart and every single one of my family members has multiple planets in Scorpio.

On the Same Page:
When Your Angles Are Aligned

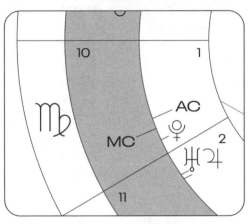

**Virgo Midheaven (MC) falling close
to Virgo ascendant (AC).**

IN THE DIAGRAM above is an example of two people having their angles fall in the same signs, which is very common with long-term couples. One partner's MC is in Virgo, which aligns with the other person's AC also in Virgo. The instances where this happens is if someone's MC/IC axis is in the same signs as your AC/DC axis, or you may both have the same AC (aka same rising signs), or you may have your AC and DC flipped, with one person being a Leo rising and the other being an Aquarius rising, for instance. Having any of these combinations means that you approach the major parts of life in a similar way. You could be very aligned on your personal goals and what you're looking for in an intimate relationship, or you could be on the same page about how to handle your home life and career.

CHAPTER 14

Shared Interests: House Overlays

nother way to assess how you and your partner relate to one another is by looking at what houses their planets fall in within your chart. When your partner's planets align with a particular house of yours, themes related to that house will show up in the relationship. The house activated can sometimes shed light on how you both met or what the main priorities are in your relationship. For example, if your partner's Venus (in the outer circle of the diagram on page 158) falls into the eleventh house of your chart (in the inner circle, indicated by the number 11), then this is an eleventh house overlay. This would mean that the two people may have been connected through friends, or they could have started the relationship as friends first before it turned romantic. Your planets activate their houses as well, so you will want to flip the two charts to see it the other way around. I've grouped the houses in which your partner's planets can fall into three distinct categories based on which ones share some common ground:

- Strong foundation houses—The first, fourth, seventh, and tenth
- Feel-good houses—The third, fifth, ninth, and eleventh
- Psychological growth houses—The second, sixth, eighth, and twelfth

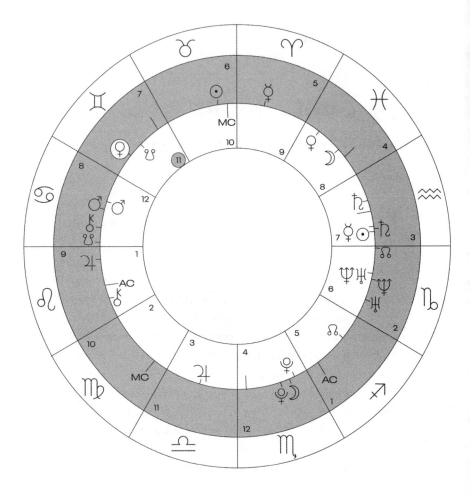

One person's Venus in Gemini falls into their partner's
eleventh house, circled in the diagram above.

You will also want to keep in mind the qualities associated with the planet that is activating a house. The sun, moon, Mercury, Venus, and Jupiter will bring comfort, optimism, and an easy, mutual understanding to that area of life, while Mars, Saturn, Uranus, Neptune, and Pluto will be harder to navigate and may bring in themes of tension, control, or instability. I would not put as much emphasis on Uranus, Neptune, and Pluto, though, because everyone of the same generation will have those planets falling in the same house.

Make a note of which houses in your chart your partner's planets activate. To start, you may want to prioritize the sun and moon, since their impact in a particular house will be the most obvious.

STRONG FOUNDATION HOUSES: FIRST, FOURTH, SEVENTH, TENTH

These four houses are the most prominent, visible parts of your chart. They also pertain to the key foundations of your life: self, home, relationships, and career. With planetary overlays in these houses, you will feel like the partnership is going somewhere and you may motivate each other to always be growing and evolving as individuals. Again, I won't be listing out what every single planet means when it falls in a house, as I want you to focus on the broader themes at play.

A partner's planets falling in your first house will influence how you express yourself. You are growing more into your true identity with the help of the other person, and you may automatically feel seen or understood by them. Meanwhile, someone's planets falling in your fourth house are ideal for starting a family or solid home life together. If a partner's planets fall into your fourth, you may be compatible roommates, or you're comfortable early on in the relationship with opening up about your deepest emotions. Someone's sun, moon, or Venus falling in the other's fourth house is a great aspect to have in a partnership, because you feel very at home in each other's presence. That person may also stimulate early childhood memories for you, or you could feel like your relationship recreates some of the patterns you had with your parents growing up, which could either be easy or difficult, depending on your relationship to your family.

With a person's planets activating your seventh house, they will embody traits that you are naturally drawn to in other people. The other person may even reflect back qualities that you need to further develop yourself. Someone's sun or moon falling in your seventh could point to an easy rapport between the two of you, while a person's Venus or Mars in your seventh means that you may find them very physically attractive.

Lastly, overlays with the tenth house in a synastry chart can indicate that one person encourages or inspires the other's work, or you might look up to your partner and admire them for how they handle themselves in public. In some cases, it can point to a relationship where you meet in the workplace or over time may notice a crossover between your two career paths. As a fun activity, check the sign that rules your tenth house and compare it to the charts of your co-workers or bosses. Chances are, they have planets that match up with that same sign ruling your tenth house.

FEEL-GOOD HOUSES: THIRD, FIFTH, NINTH, ELEVENTH

The third, fifth, ninth, and eleventh are my favorite houses to have activated in synastry charts. I call them the "feel-good" houses because, when someone's planets are positioned in these parts of your chart, you may light up when you're around them, or they could just automatically understand your unique point of view and who you are at your core. In the case of third and ninth house overlays, it is easy to converse with the other person and they may inspire you to keep an open mind to different beliefs and ways of thinking about the world. You're never at a loss for what to say around each other, and you could have a similar sense of humor. Additionally, they may encourage you to go after what ignites your curiosity, or the two of you could make great travel partners. It may even be that you met while traveling somewhere.

If someone's planets activate your fifth house, you may find them very fun to be around, and they may urge you to lean into your creative skills and be more confident in what you have to say and offer. Having eleventh house overlays will bring that same light-hearted, friendly quality. You and your partner may run in similar communities or social circles, or you could have started off the relationship as friends. Outside of romantic relationships, you may find that your good friends also have planets that fall into your fifth or eleventh houses, since these houses are primarily about socializing and having a good time.

PSYCHOLOGICAL GROWTH HOUSES: SECOND, SIXTH, EIGHTH, TWELFTH
The second, sixth, eighth, and twelfth houses tend to be a bit trickier, because when someone's planets fall in these parts of your chart, they are hidden from your ascendant and descendant, meaning that they do not form an aspect to these angles. Placements here can also stir up uncomfortable emotions, because they urge you to face the buried parts of yourself. The sixth and the twelfth are both houses that revolve around being of service to others. Activations to the sixth house may make you feel like you have to constantly support your partner, and you could give a lot of your energy away to helping them through their problems or accommodating their lifestyle. With twelfth house overlays, especially if it's the other person's sun or moon that falls in your twelfth house, it may be hard to get a grasp on who that person really is—you don't always "get" them as a person. There may also be a lack of trust in the relationship. However, on a more positive note, when someone's planets fall in your sixth or twelfth house, the relationship may promote healing and inner growth within yourself. Your partner may set you off on a spiritual awakening, or you could come to terms with self-sabotaging patterns that you need to release.

With eighth house planetary overlays, you may encounter control issues in the relationship, or the other person may help you to confront deeper psychological problems. In addition, it may simply be that you get emotionally intimate very early on, or finances and sharing resources are big topics that come up in the relationship. To give a non-romantic example, I have a friend who I collaborate with on creating astrology courses, and her Saturn falls into my eighth house. Rather than simply being friends, we also have to manage money we make together and split our earnings down the middle. Someone's planets falling into your second house will bring in themes of work and money as well, and it could be that you work together, or you want to start a business and build something concrete as a couple. This house can bring up feelings of possessiveness, though, so be wary of trying to exert too much control over your partner, and vice versa.

PART FOUR

What Does the Future Hold for You?

Timing Relationship Activity

By now, we have a sound understanding of both your birth chart and synastry chart. As a reminder, your birth chart never changes; it will remain the same throughout your entire life. However, there will be days, months, and years when parts of your birth chart become more emphasized, and time periods in which the potential of certain planets or houses will be fully awakened. Transit charts indicate when specific parts of your chart are activated and are a fundamental technique of predictive astrology.

Predicting events is personally my favorite part of astrology. I am someone who has the tendency to worry a lot, panicking that I don't feel completely in control of the future. In my early twenties, I used to compare myself to other people my age, worrying that they were so much further ahead in their careers while I was still at assistant level. I would also be hard on myself for not being in a relationship, because it felt like everyone was either dating or coupled up. My mindset was that if I just worked harder at my career or swiped on enough dating apps, I would be more successful, and I would have a boyfriend. If I wasn't constantly trying to get ahead in some area of my life, I wasn't doing enough. Learning predictive astrology helped me to chill out and realize that there is a specific timing for every event in your life. Everyone really is on their own unique timeline, so it's not worth comparing yourself to others.

Understanding transits not only helped me feel calmer about my future, but it also allowed me to make peace with my past. I could look back at certain dates and recognize that there was nothing I could have done differently to avoid a particular situation; it was simply meant to happen at that moment in time. Though learning about my birth chart placements helped me embrace parts of my personality I had always struggled with, teaching myself how to read transits is what ultimately got me to accept where I currently am in life, rather than blaming myself for not doing enough.

Learning transits is our final step in piecing together the various parts of relationship astrology. Understanding timing is so crucial, because in order for a solid relationship to form, the stars have to align at the same moment for both people. You could have great astrological compatibility with someone, but it doesn't end up working out simply because it's not the right time for you to be in a relationship. As we go over how to read transits and apply them to your chart throughout this next section, I hope that by the end you, too, will be able to trust your individual timing.

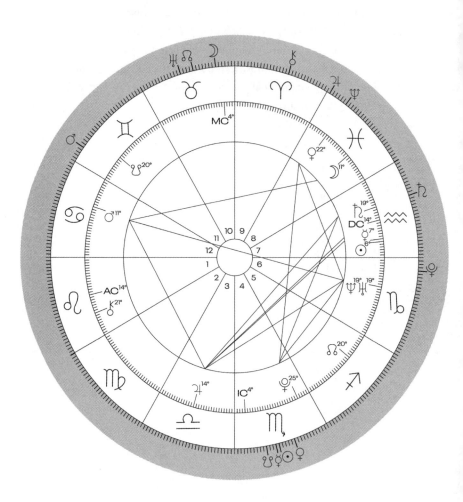

An example of a transit chart.
The transiting planets on the outside move in a
counterclockwise direction around your birth chart.

CHAPTER 15

An Introduction
to Transit Charts

et's dive deeper into understanding how transits work—I'm excited for you to start putting them into practice! Transits show where the planets currently are in the sky, which you can then overlay onto your individual birth chart, to see how a specific day, month, or year will go for you.

For instance, maybe you have a couple of planets in your second house, signaling that you have the potential to make good money for yourself or be an entrepreneur, but you're at the start of your career and have yet to see that happen. By looking at transits in relation to your birth chart and tracking when they move into your second house, you will be able to predict what month or year you might receive a boost in finances or see growth in terms of starting your own business.

You may also hear from friends or on social media about events like Uranus, Saturn, or Pluto moving into specific signs and what that means for the world at large. At the time of this book's publication, Pluto will have just begun its 20-year transit through the sign of Aquarius. Everyone will be feeling this planetary cycle, but when you look at where that transit of Pluto moving through Aquarius falls in your individual birth chart, you will see how it uniquely impacts your own life.

The diagram to the left shows the transiting planets in the outer circle (for the date November 7, 2022, as I'm writing this), with a regular birth chart in the middle. As the transits move around the birth chart at varying speeds, going in a counterclockwise direction, they will move through specific houses in your chart, passing over any planets and angles in those houses. The house, planet, or angle in your chart that the transit planets activate will give you an idea of what part of life is currently being emphasized. Transits can show things like when you might experience career expansion, move homes, or have a change in a relationship. You can also look to transits to determine when you might go through challenging periods in your life versus when you might have an amazing year. Throughout this next section, we will be learning how to track when transits affect the relationship-oriented parts of your chart, like your seventh house, moon, and Venus, so you can get an idea of when you might enter into a new relationship, experience a happy event in an existing relationship, or go through a period of stress, or even a break-up.

How to start tracking your transits

1. **PULL UP YOUR TRANSIT CHART.** To familiarize yourself with transits, I recommend pulling up your transit chart on the websites astro.com or astro-seek.com. These websites should be your best friends by now. On astro.com, select "Natal Chart and Transits" on the Chart Type drop-down menu. You can then enter in whatever date you want to look at. On astro-seek.com, "Transit Chart" is an option on the sidebar of the page when viewing your birth chart, or it can be found on the "charts, calculations" drop-down menu at the top left of the home page. I personally prefer using astro-seek.com to look at transits because you can click forward and backward in time to get a better visual of how the planets move at different speeds around your chart.

2. **TAKE NOTE OF WHERE THE TRANSIT PLANETS ARE FALLING AROUND YOUR BIRTH CHART.** As you familiarize yourself with looking at a transit chart, draw your eye to which houses and signs in your birth chart the transit planets are activating. For example, you might notice that the moon on the day you are reading this is located on the outer ring of your third house in the sign of Leo. You may even want to write this information down, so you can easily refer back to it as you read ahead.

3. **PLAY AROUND WITH VARIOUS DATES.** Over the next few chapters, we will be looking at transits that indicate relationship activity, so you may want to go back to the transits for specific dates, such as when you got into a relationship, were dating a lot more, or simply formed a meaningful connection with someone, no matter how short or how long that relationship was. If it was significant to you, it is worth noting. You can also do the same for dates when you went through a break-up or a stressful period in a relationship.

4. **NOTE HOW THE PLANETS MOVE AT VARYING SPEEDS.** As you move forward and backward in time, plugging in different dates to the transit chart, you will notice how certain planets move quickly through each sign and house, while others take their sweet time. The difference in the movements between planets might be easier to see if you go day by day, looking at just how far the planets move through a sign and a house of your chart.

Before we fully get into tracking transits, I want to make it clear what they can and cannot determine. When I give readings, people sometimes presume I'm looking into a crystal ball and seeing every single detail of what their future might hold. However, transits just show the potential for what might happen, as well as the energy surrounding a specific time period. You may have an idea of what is in store for you, but you can never entirely predict what exact event may occur. Going back to the theme of relationships, for example, transits can show when a happy period for a relationship might occur. What you won't be able to see is what that specific happy event is, or who it is with (if you aren't already coupled up). It could be that you're meeting someone, moving in with your partner, getting married, or having a child together. It all depends on your current life circumstances at the time the transit takes place. The same goes for periods of relationship stress. Though transits can show when you may feel distant from your partner or have some tension come up in the relationship, they cannot definitively show if a break-up will occur. The decision to end a relationship is still entirely up to you.

It is also important to keep in mind that the planets aren't forcing anything upon you or causing random events to happen out of nowhere. Typically, the planetary transits to your chart echo what you are already feeling deep down in your gut. For example, you may have a transit come along that indicates a job change, but in the weeks leading up to that you may have started to feel the pull to go in a new direction with work. Or it might be that a transit for getting into a relationship comes along, and you had just decided to keep an open mind when dating and let love into your life. If you are truly listening to yourself, then you already know the answers, but what is helpful about predictive astrology is that it gives you a solid time period to look out for, when a change might take place or a new opportunity may arise. While I also use other timing techniques to track life events in my own practice, I consider transits to be the key starting point in learning how to predict. If something major is happening in your life, it can always be found in the transit chart.

Planets in Transit

IN THE FIRST section of this book, we went over what each planet means in the context of your birth chart. When we are studying transits, though, the meanings of these planets are slightly different. As I mentioned before, the planets move at varying speeds through the zodiac in a counterclockwise motion (except for the Nodes, which move clockwise). If you're using whole sign houses, the planetary transits through a specific sign correlate with the transits through one house as well. The second a planet moves into a different sign, it automatically moves into a different house of your chart. A planet in transit will bring its unique signification to an area of your life for a set amount of time.

In the case of the moon, which spends two and a half days in a sign and takes about 28 days to make a lap through all 12 signs, you will feel its transit very briefly. Your emotions, symbolized by the moon, will be tied to a specific area of your life, like work, family, or relationships, for just a day or two. Meanwhile, other planets have much longer transits. Saturn spends two and a half to three years in a single sign, taking about 29 years to make its way through the whole zodiac. Therefore, a Saturn transit through a sign and a house will be felt over an extended period of time. The Saturnian influence of learning hard lessons, restructuring, or taking on greater responsibility and commitments will taint a particular area of your life for a three-year period. Pluto has the longest transit of all, spending anywhere from 12–30 years in one single sign and taking about 248 years to go through the whole zodiac. It may take you until the end of a two-decade long Pluto transit to notice how much transformation you've undergone in that specific area. I've put the time frame each of these planets spend in a single sign (and therefore house) below the description of each transit.

I know this is a lot of information, so the best starting point for observing how transits play out in your own life is by simply tracking the transit of the sun and moon through your chart every day. Both of these planets move pretty quickly, so by following them consistently, you can see what type of events may occur or what kind of mindset you're in when they go through a specific house or over a planet in your chart. You will then begin to get an idea of what a transit feels like to that part of your chart in general.

Pull up your transit chart now and note what house and sign each planet is currently moving through. Then read the following.

SUN: The sun's transit indicates what zodiac "season" it currently is. If it is Scorpio season, for instance, you will automatically know that the sun is transiting through Scorpio. The transit sun shows where you are growing as a person and tapping into different sides of your identity. It also indicates what goals and interests might be the most important to you over a month-long period. For example, the sun moving through your fifth house might show that you are focused on building creative projects, or you're busier with dating and seeing friends for a few weeks. Meanwhile, the sun transiting your ninth house would mean that you are traveling internationally, taking a course, or doing extensive reading and research on your own time for about a month.
TIME SPENT IN EACH SIGN: 30 days.

MOON: The moon's transit indicates where your feelings lie, as well as where you might be experiencing emotional highs and lows over a two-day period. It also shows where more minor events are happening on a day-to-day basis. For example, if you feel motivated to exercise one day, the moon might be moving through your sixth house, while if you are getting paid for a recent work project you've done, the moon might be transiting your second house.
TIME SPENT IN EACH SIGN: Two and a half days.

MERCURY: Mercury transits point to what you're the most curious about for a period of a few weeks. Mercury shows what is weighing on your mind and what topics you will want to research or discuss in more depth with people. It can also indicate what types of details you're handling or the quality of conversations you're having. For example, Mercury transiting the fourth house may mean important conversations are taking place within your family, while Mercury transiting the tenth house may mean that you're thinking about your career ambitions or talking to your boss about taking on more responsibilities.

TIME SPENT IN EACH SIGN: about three weeks, but up to two months when retrograde.

VENUS: Venus transits often indicate where you are receiving praise, what you're indulging in, or in which area you're developing a positive outlook. Venus transits can also bring up romance and social activity and influence how you're expressing love and affection during a specific period. Additionally, Venus transits point to where you are working to achieve greater balance and harmony. Venus transiting the seventh house may bring peace and greater romance to your relationships, while Venus transiting the third house may mean you're enjoying a pleasant bit of travel or you're spending more time reading and writing.

TIME SPENT IN EACH SIGN: about three to four weeks, but up to four months when retrograde.

MARS: Mars transits show where you're putting your energy and what is motivating you during a set period. Mars can also show what areas you're encountering conflict in, or where you're learning how to be more independent. In some instances, a Mars transit can symbolize cutting ties or breaking free from any restrictions you've felt in areas of your life. It urges you to take action. Mars transiting your first house would make you more assertive about your own goals and standing up for yourself, while Mars moving through your tenth house may have you quitting one job for another.

TIME IT SPENDS IN EACH SIGN: about six weeks but can be up to seven months when retrograde.

Retrograde planets

I haven't mentioned retrograde planets yet, but they become very relevant in the context of transits. Every planet, except the sun and moon, goes retrograde. Looking at a transit chart, you can spot when a planet is retrograde, because it will move backward against the flow of the other planets for however long its retrograde lasts. When a planet is retrograde, it will remain in a sign and a house for a longer period of time than it normally would.

Mercury retrograde typically happens three times a year for three weeks at a time, Venus retrograde happens once every 18 months for 40 days at a time but can be up to four months because of its retrograde cycle. Mars retrograde occurs once every two years for about two and a half months at a time but can be up to seven months because of its retrograde cycle, and Jupiter, Saturn, Uranus, Neptune, and Pluto are all retrograde for about three to four months every single year. Themes that come up during retrograde periods often involve slowing down, doing greater reflection, and revisiting something or someone from the past.

The meaning of whatever planet is retrograde also becomes more of a focus during that time; in the case of Mercury, it's often about how you communicate, and with Venus it's about how you approach relationships.

♃ **JUPITER:** Jupiter transits are indicative of where you're experiencing the most growth and optimism for a year-long period. Jupiter tends to bring up positive opportunities that don't require as much effort to receive. It also gives you the feeling that you're gaining new knowledge or developing more of an open mind in the area of life that it's activating. On the other hand, Jupiter transits can also show where you're breaking free of restriction, as well as where you may feel overwhelmed or are prone to overdoing it. Jupiter transiting the eleventh house can mean frequent social activities or feeling like you're being supported by a group of people, but you may also feel like you don't have any time to yourself. Meanwhile, Jupiter transiting the sixth house may result in positive work opportunities, but you could also feel overwhelmed by your everyday tasks.

TIME IT SPENDS IN EACH SIGN: about one year.

♄ **SATURN:** Saturn transits urge you to restructure a certain area of your life and lay a solid foundation that can better serve you in the long term. However, this is not always easy, and Saturn transiting through a particular house or over a planet can bring up a lot of stress as you face the harsh reality of certain situations. Saturn can also point to which area of life is stressing you out the most, where you may feel weighed down by responsibilities or limited in some way. However, Saturn transits ultimately serve to show you who and what is worth committing to, and by the end of its transit through a sign and house you may feel like you have a mastery over that area of your life that you didn't three years prior. For example, Saturn transiting the second house may bring up financial stress, but it could mean you are building your own business or getting serious about budgeting your money. On the other hand, Saturn transiting the seventh house may have you reevaluating your relationships and getting serious about what types of people you want to commit to.

TIME IT SPENDS IN EACH SIGN: around two and a half to three years.

Your Saturn Return

The most well-known Saturn transit is called the Saturn Return, which is when Saturn returns to the position it was in when you were born. Because Saturn spends around two and a half to three years in a sign, it takes about 29 years to make its "return." Therefore, at the age of 29 (sometimes a bit earlier, sometimes a bit later, depending on the chart of the individual), themes pertaining to Saturn become especially relevant. You may have the sudden urge to level up in an area of your life or break free from the ways in which you've been holding yourself back up until that point. You're establishing yourself as your own individual in the world, so if there's an area where you haven't been living true to yourself, it will become increasingly obvious. Oftentimes, bigger career, home and relationship changes happen as a result of the Saturn return. This transit also repeats in your late fifties and late eighties, so you will want to pay attention to those ages as well.

URANUS: Uranus transits tend to be unpredictable. They are neither challenging nor easy, they just bring up events and situations that you didn't quite anticipate. Uranus also speeds things up, so when it transits through a particular house or over a planet in your chart, you may notice quick changes coming into effect. You may also want to go against the status quo and approach that area of your life in a completely different way to how you may have previously. You will want to break free of societal expectations and have greater independence and freedom there. However, that part of your life may feel a bit unstable, or you could experience some nervous energy. For instance, Uranus transiting through the tenth house often means a change in career path or a desire to work independently, while Uranus transiting over your moon would indicate moving homes quickly or having unexpected changes take place within your family.

TIME IT SPENDS IN EACH SIGN: about seven to eight years.

NEPTUNE: Neptune transits can cause a lot of confusion. Because it takes so long to move through a house and sign in your chart, Neptune transits are most noticeable when they move into an aspect with one of the planets or angles in your chart. Whatever part of your chart it is activating is probably an area where you're not entirely sure of how to structure your life or what you want for yourself. You may have pent-up frustration about a situation, but you're not sure of the best way forward until Neptune moves away from the exact degree of a planet or angle. On a more positive note, Neptune transits serve to soften you up and make you more compassionate and giving. They can also boost creativity or spirituality and make you hyperaware of everything going on around you. On the one hand, Neptune moving across your descendant line or over your Venus may leave you feeling uncertain of where you stand in a romantic relationship. On the other hand, it could also present a fairy-tale romance type of situation, where you're opening your heart up to someone new.

TIME IT SPENDS IN EACH SIGN: about 14 years.

PLUTO: Pluto transits typically bring up deep, inner transformation. Similar to Neptune, a Pluto transit will be most noticeable when it aspects a planet or angle in your chart to the exact degree, which lasts for about a year or two. Pluto can also bring themes related to death and rebirth, so under its transit you may feel like you're shedding an old version of yourself and uncovering hidden sides of your identity. It may also mean that you are experiencing literal loss in your life and learning how to better let go. Additionally, Pluto transits indicate where you might be encountering power struggles, or areas in which you're interested in doing in-depth research. Pluto transiting across your ascendant line or over your sun may transform your appearance and how you want to present yourself to the world, while Pluto transiting over your Venus may help you to heal old relationship patterns but could also bring up control issues in a relationship.

TIME IT SPENDS IN EACH SIGN: anywhere between 12–30 years in a sign. Pluto has an irregular transit, spending the most time in Taurus and the least time in Scorpio.

THE NORTH AND SOUTH NODES: The Nodes move against the direction of all the other planets in transit, going in a clockwise direction. Whatever signs the Nodes are transiting through indicates where the solar and lunar eclipses are currently taking place. The Nodes always transit a pair of two signs that are directly opposite to one another. So, for example, if the North Node is transiting through Taurus, you will automatically know that the South Node is transiting through Scorpio. The transit of the North Node points to what you are working on developing further but can also represent what you're still a little uncomfortable with. Meanwhile, South Node transits show what area you need to release negative mindsets around and urge you to overcome past patterns holding you back in that part of your life. For example, the North Node transiting through the sixth house will have you wanting to find greater structure at work, find a new job, or get more serious about your physical health, while the simultaneous transit of the South Node through your twelfth house is asking you to release any self-sabotaging patterns and tend to any mental health concerns.

TIME SPENT IN A PAIR OF SIGNS: about 18 months.

CHIRON: Chiron's transits often symbolize where you are working through deep-seated wounds and anxieties. Wherever it is transiting in your chart is an area that you are actively healing. When Chiron moves over a specific planet in your chart, you could encounter tough emotional experiences that involve the signification of that planet. For instance, Chiron transiting over your moon may bring up painful feelings surrounding your family or an intimate relationship. Meanwhile, Chiron transiting your eleventh house may bring up anxiety around your friendships, or you may join a community that helps you to heal.

TIME SPENT IN EACH SIGN: anywhere from one to nine years in a sign. Chiron has an irregular transit and spends the most time in Aries and the least time in Libra.

When you are looking at transits, you will want to take note of their movement through the houses, as well as when a transit planet passes right over a planet or angle in your chart. I have listed the time frame each planet spends in a sign (and therefore house), but when a transit is exactly conjunct (moving directly on top of) a specific planet or angle in your chart, note that the slower outer planets like Saturn, Uranus, Neptune, and Pluto will typically spend a year or two in that position. The time transits spend moving through houses and across angles and planets are all important to take into consideration when we are determining relationship timing, because it shows how long the opening might be for a significant relationship to form, as well as how long a period of relationship stress may last.

CHAPTER 16

Tracking Relationship Highs and Lows: The Transits of Jupiter, Saturn, and the Nodes

I wish I had known about my difficult astrological transits during my twenties, and that it simply was not the right time for me to meet anyone. I didn't have a strong sense of self, I wasn't quite sure of where I wanted to be in my long-term career, and I put every guy I dated on a pedestal, thinking that he had it all figured out and could somehow step in and save me from myself. I was desperate for every guy I dated to like me, without ever stepping back to consider whether I even liked them. An understanding of astrology would have saved me so much time, energy, and heartbreak. Once I learned how to read transits in my astrological chart, I was able to shift my focus away from obsessively dating to other areas of my life, such as health, work, or family relationships. Even though I was by that time in my late twenties and had never been in a relationship that had lasted longer than three months, I no longer felt like such a failure when it came to love. I knew that eventually the planets would align and give me a significant relationship. And as I mentioned in the introduction, that's exactly what happened. So yes, all of this timing stuff I'm about to show you really does work.

Now that we have the basics down for interpreting transits, let's go over what you should be looking out for when you're trying to time relationship activity for yourself. This is the part of astrology that has brought me the most peace of mind. Before I knew how to read my chart, I used to spend a lot of time aimlessly swiping on dating apps or trying to analyze why a guy wasn't being as responsive as I would have liked. I used to make myself feel physically ill worrying about whether it was going to work out with someone I hardly knew. If this sounds familiar to you, or you're currently going through challenging times in your love life, I've put this chapter together to help you.

We're going to focus on transits that indicate when it is more likely that you will enter into a relationship with someone and have significant relationship growth. These planetary movements could indicate a time when you're making the relationship official, moving in with your partner, getting married, or simply feeling closer than you have in the past. Sometimes it may be that a person meets their life partner during these openings, while in other cases it could be that they have a relationship which may not last in the long term but is still very significant to them and their personal growth. There is no one-size-fits-all with these transits. In addition, it's important to note that just because you have these transits occurring doesn't mean the universe is going to bring you the relationship of your dreams if you aren't open to receiving it. If you continue to tell yourself that you aren't worthy of love or you're repeatedly attracted to people who are emotionally unavailable, these transits will most likely bring a romantic situation into your life that reflects the way you treat yourself. Astrology is simply presenting you with the energy to form a meaningful relationship at a given time, but it is up to you to decide how you're going to work with it.

We'll also discuss how these same transits can signal a time of break-up. There is a dual quality to each planet's transit through your chart, so it's important to look at how you're feeling about your partner when the exact timing is happening. If you sense that a relationship is not good for you and it's something you have been trying to walk away from for a while, these same planetary cycles can be a time when you decide to separate.

In the previous chapter, I went over what each planet means in transit. Now I want to zoom in on three of those transits specifically: Jupiter, Saturn, and the North and South Nodes. These are the most critical to keep an eye on when timing relationship activity. Why are these transits more important than all of the others? Each of these planets (or in the case of the Nodes, mathematical points) spends enough time in a particular part of your chart to make more of a lasting impact. Rather than the shorter transits of the sun or Venus through a house and sign, which only last several weeks, Saturn, Jupiter, and the Nodes take between one to three years to cycle through that part of your chart. Therefore, you're able to see significant growth and developments take place within your relationships over a longer period of time. These transits also don't come around often, so when they do occur, they bring the potential to form a more meaningful, lasting partnership. Yes, Uranus, Neptune, and Pluto have long transits as well, but to be honest they're too long. It's hard to pinpoint exact years when a relationship development will take place when you're looking at those transits, because they last between eight and 30 years! The potential effects of Uranus, Neptune, and Pluto transits tend to lie dormant until Jupiter, Saturn, or the Nodes come along to awaken their full potential.

A Make-It-or-Break-It Period: Saturn Transits

I CONSIDER SATURN to be the most important planet to track when timing significant relationships, because Saturn symbolizes commitment, stability, and putting in the work to make a partnership last. However, Saturn can also indicate feelings of stress, separation, and emotional heaviness. Therefore, Saturn transiting the relationship-oriented parts of your chart often signals a make-or-break period for a partnership, where you're figuring out if a relationship is worth your effort and deciding if it has the potential to go the distance.

Saturn spends about two and a half to three years in a sign and house, and it takes roughly 29 years to make its way around your entire chart. Because of its slow movement, when it passes through a relationship house or aspects one of the inner planets in your chart, particularly the sun, moon, or Venus, you may find yourself reevaluating your love life and figuring out how you can restructure a certain mindset or patterns in this area. If you've been dating and haven't wanted to settle down with anyone up until this point, a Saturn transit will often present an opportunity to experience greater commitment with a partner. Suddenly, you may want a long-term relationship, and it could be frustrating to keep seeing someone who isn't as serious as you are. You will find it difficult to keep things casual with people.

SATURN TRANSITING THE SEVENTH HOUSE

First and foremost, I want to look at Saturn's transit through your seventh house. This is a period of up to three years that urges you to face the reality of certain relationships. If you've been going about dating in a certain way up until this point, you may want to step back and look at any patterns you might be repeating. For those who are single at the start of a Saturn seventh house transit, you can expect a lot more relationship activity to come up. Right before this transit, Saturn would have spent three years in your sixth house, where work and wellness were your two main priorities. There may have been little time to date, or it just wasn't a huge priority for you, but as soon as Saturn crosses into the seventh house, you will notice your love life becoming more of a focus. Even if you don't meet your partner immediately, you will most likely still have dating experiences that urge you to get more serious about what type of relationship you want. However, Saturn's transit through your seventh house won't allow you to date just anyone, and you may find yourself dissatisfied with any relationship that doesn't have long-lasting potential. It could also be that situationships or people who aren't ultimately right for you will fall away at this time. Another result of this transit is that you end up building greater confidence when dating. Over the course of Saturn's three years in your seventh house, you are getting clearer on what you want out of a partner, as well as understanding the negative habits you want to eliminate when it comes to dating and relationships.

If you are already coupled up when Saturn enters your seventh house, you may find yourself wanting to deepen your commitment to your partner. You might decide to move in with someone or get engaged or married. You will be urged to take that next step with your partner, and you may end up having conversations about what the future looks like together. On the other hand, Saturn can often introduce stress into existing relationships, which is why this transit can also signify break-ups. During this transit, you may have to put more effort into the relationship. Your partner may go through a stressful period where they need your support, or you may encounter challenges as a couple that you have to overcome together. It's not uncommon to feel a bit distant from your partner during this time. Saturn also asks you to improve upon your partnership skills and consider the needs of someone else. If there is one person who is doing all of the heavy lifting in the relationship, this will become increasingly obvious. When Saturn is moving through your seventh house, you are seeing a relationship for what it really is, not what you wish it could be.

OTHER NOTABLE SATURN TRANSITS

Other Saturn transits are not as obvious but can still result in a significant relationship. In addition to Saturn transiting the seventh house, its movement through the first and eighth houses is important to note, too. Because the first and seventh houses are opposite to one another, any transit through the first house automatically influences the seventh house. A first house Saturn transit is similar to a seventh house one, in that it's also a period where you are getting more serious about who and what you commit to, and you may want to take on greater responsibilities in your personal life, such as taking the next step in a partnership. The transit of Saturn through your first house has its fair share of difficulties, too, and can sometimes signify a time where you have to become more self-reliant after a relationship ends. You might also be uncovering different sides to your identity and realizing that a current relationship is no longer serving you.

Meanwhile, Saturn moving through your eighth house takes relationships to the next level. If your relationship was established during Saturn's transit of your seventh house or even earlier, the three years that follow in the eighth will be about combining finances, learning how to be more vulnerable, and sharing the messier parts of your lives with each other. Whether you're in a relationship or not, you could also need to work through any psychological issues you have with intimacy. You will be taking a closer look at how you approach conflict within your relationships, and eliminating any patterns or mindsets that are working against you.

Less intense Saturn transits that are also great for establishing relationships include Saturn moving through your third, fifth, ninth, and eleventh houses. These four houses are all relational houses, so they deal with how you interact and communicate with other people. The eleventh house has to do with groups, friends, and a bigger sense of community, while the third house pertains to those social connections you form in your nearby environment, such as neighbors or friends whom you meet up with on a regular basis. The fifth house is about how you balance your own needs while interacting with others, so a lot of the time Saturn transiting the fifth house is about building greater self-esteem when dating or feeling comfortable putting yourself out there. Lastly, the ninth house is about your core beliefs and having eye-opening new experiences through learning and travel. Interactions with people from foreign countries or who hold different opinions help to shape your unique views on the world. When Saturn transits through each of these houses, it signals a time of greater relationship activity and feeling more connected to others.

This doesn't always include romantic relationships, though, and in some cases, it may just be that you're learning how to be a better friend or taking on greater responsibilities in group settings.

SATURN TRANSITING YOUR INNER PLANETS

In addition to Saturn's transits through the above houses, it will also be important to note when a transiting Saturn makes an aspect to certain planets in your chart, looking specifically at the sun, moon, and Venus. In the diagram below, you can see transit Saturn forming a conjunction to the moon in someone's chart. When Saturn forms a conjunction, square, opposition, or trine to any of these planets, lessons that pertain to the core meaning of each of those planets become more prominent in a person's life. (If you need a refresher on how to identify aspects in your chart, see page 87.) The trine tends to be much easier to handle and signifies relationships coming easily, while the conjunction, square, and opposition may be more difficult to go through but tend to lead to life-changing lessons within relationships.

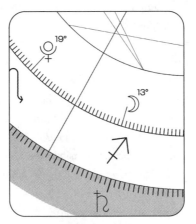

**Transit Saturn forming
a conjunction to the moon.**

When Saturn forms an aspect to your moon, you may have to reflect on how you are voicing your feelings in your relationships. This transit tends to bring up early home life and past conditioning, so you may become more aware of how you're repeating childhood patterns when you're with your partner. Because the moon can also represent the physical home space, transit Saturn in an aspect to your moon may mean that there is a significant move taking place, too, such as living with someone for the first time and learning how to share your space. Meanwhile, when Saturn forms an aspect to your Venus, you may become a lot more selective about who you date. You may start dating just one person, or this could be a period where a serious milestone is reached in an existing relationship. On the other hand, it can bring to the surface any ways in which a relationship might be off balance. In addition to romantic situations, a Saturn transit of your Venus may have you cutting back on socializing or weeding out friends who don't have your best interests at heart. You would rather spend your energy strengthening the friendships and romantic connections that mean the most to you.

Throughout this book, I haven't really said much about the sun in your chart in regard to relationships. However, the sun becomes more significant in your love life when there are longer transits aspecting it, like Saturn. The sun represents our sense of self and our identity, so when Saturn transits your sun, it urges you to figure out who you really are, and it's often through relationships that you are able to see yourself more clearly. Saturn transiting the sun urges you to reevaluate what responsibilities you want to take on and also asks you to narrow down who and what you commit to. You might be met with limitations in certain areas of your life during this transit, as you realize that you can't say yes to absolutely everything.

Relationship Happiness and Growth: Jupiter Transits

WHILE SATURN TRANSITS through certain parts of your chart can either result in greater commitment or additional stress in a relationship, Jupiter transits for the most part are easy. When Jupiter transits through houses like the first, fifth or seventh or aspects your sun, moon, or Venus, you typically experience a happy period in your relationship, or you might be approaching dating in a more open-minded, optimistic way. These same Jupiter transits can also result in heightened social activity, so it is more likely that you will have opportunities to meet new people and establish relationships, both romantic and platonic. If you have felt lonely before Jupiter makes its way to these houses and planets I mention below, that feeling of isolation will usually lift. You will not only feel good about your love life, but also about who you are in general.

Jupiter does have its downsides, though. Sometimes, its transits can amplify existing problems in a relationship or mark a period where you're breaking free from a romantic situation that feels restrictive. That being said, we will be looking at Jupiter transits that are good for meeting a significant partner and achieving better dating success, as well as those that can sometimes result in a break-up or feeling distant from your partner.

As a reminder, Jupiter takes about 12 years to make its way through all signs and houses in your chart, spending one year in each. Because it moves much more quickly than Saturn, you will be able to identify similar patterns that arise every time it transits through specific areas of your chart.

JUPITER'S HOUSE TRANSITS

I want to start off with Jupiter's transits through your first and seventh houses. As Jupiter makes its way through these parts of your chart, you will often experience better luck in relationships. With Jupiter transiting through the seventh house, you may end up meeting someone significant if you're single, or you could be making more of an effort to put yourself out there in the dating scene. If you happen to already be coupled up at the start of this transit, you may feel much closer to your partner or have a momentous event occur, like getting married or having a child together. Additionally, you may establish other partnerships and close friendships, and find it easy to connect one-on-one with people.

To differentiate between the first and seventh transits of Jupiter, Jupiter moving through your first house tends to be a more self-focused time, where you may feel sure of your next life steps and confident in who you are. Additionally, you may notice that you're receiving attention from other people in general, whether that be at work or in your love life. It's almost like this newly gained sense of confidence results in people being romantically drawn to you. Though these Jupiter transits tend to be mostly positive, they can also signify a time when you will want greater personal freedom. If you've been in a relationship that is weighing you down or doesn't fit with who you are anymore, then you may have the desire to break free of it and be on your own.

I also wanted to mention Jupiter's transits through your fifth and eleventh houses. Though, on their own and without the help of a simultaneous Saturn or Nodal transit, these transits are unlikely to result in anything major happening in a relationship, they are still great times for dating more frequently. Jupiter's transit of your fifth house is a year-long period where you may have an abundance of romantic prospects and are also realizing your self-worth when it comes to relationships. You will likely be learning how to make your own interests more of a priority, rather than completely losing your sense of identity with the people you date. Meanwhile, Jupiter moving through your eleventh house will serve to widen your social network, and there may be many more opportunities to get out of the house and meet new people.

There are two Jupiter transits in particular that I frequently see at the time of break-ups. If you're in a relationship and you see these coming up, I wouldn't get anxious, though. These transits don't automatically mean a break-up, but when two people decide to part ways it's likely that one of them is occurring. Jupiter transiting through your eighth house will urge you to go deeper in your relationship and will open you up to sharing money or greater intimacy with your partner. However, it can also amplify existing relationship problems, and you may have to put more effort in to resolve them. One person may want greater commitment, while the other could still be holding back. Alternatively, Jupiter's transit through your twelfth house is a period where you may be spending more time alone or feel distant from other people, including your partner. It can also be a year when you deal with mental health struggles and find that a lot of suppressed emotions come up, which can sometimes prove to be a challenge in an existing relationship.

JUPITER'S TRANSITS TO YOUR PLANETS

When transit Jupiter makes an aspect to a particular planet in your chart, it amplifies the qualities associated with that planet, making it more prominent in your life for about a year-long period. Of course, it's important to note the date that Jupiter reaches an exact conjunction, square, or opposition to one of your planets, because that is when the transit will be felt the strongest. The house placement of that particular planet will be relevant in interpreting how the overall transit will go. In general, though, Jupiter aspecting your sun tends to bring more attention to you, and you may be met with positive opportunities, both at work and in your personal life. You're doing important self-discovery and feeling confident in letting your full personality shine around other people. So, while this transit may often signify getting a big promotion at work or starting interesting projects, it also can point to entering into an exciting new relationship chapter.

Jupiter transits to your moon will have you focused on expressing your emotions differently. You may find it easier to up and be vulnerable with a romantic partner at this time, or the fact that you are dating someone new and that requires you to become comfortable sharing the sensitive, more hidden sides of yourself. Because the moon also signifies the literal home, I see Jupiter–moon transits going on when two people move in together, buy a house, or expand their family by having a baby. Home and family become a bigger focus for that specific year. On the downside, though, this transit can also be a period of emotional highs and lows, where your feelings are magnified. Any emotions you would normally keep buried are brought to the surface for you to work through.

Jupiter aspecting Venus is one of my favorite transits. It often marks a period where you are socializing more frequently or having success with dating. If you're already in a relationship, you may feel in sync with your partner or you're optimistic about the next steps you're taking together as a couple. There is another side to this transit that is not entirely related to love where you could also receive more money at work or feel less stressed about finances.

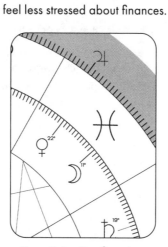

**Transit Jupiter forming
a conjunction to Venus.**

Change Is Coming:
North and South Node Transits

WE HAVE JUST learned that Saturn transits tend to bring a serious tone to a relationship and often symbolize a make-or-break time for a couple, while Jupiter transits bring up positive relationship events and optimism about a couple's future together. When it comes to the transits of the North and South Nodes, you can always know that change is coming. When applied to the realm of relationships, these changes, symbolized by the Nodal transits, might mean going from being single to in a relationship, or from being in a relationship to single. It could also be that the dynamic between you and your partner is simply shifting, or certain elements of the relationship are changing. An example would be one person suddenly having a more demanding career or needing to travel for work frequently, so the couple needs to make sure they are prioritizing the time they do have together.

To reiterate, the Nodes move clockwise through the signs, so they will be moving in the opposite direction to which all of the other planets are headed. The Nodes spend about 18 months transiting through one house and one sign of your chart, so when they are moving through a relationship-oriented house, for instance, changes to a relationship can take place at any point during this year-and-a-half period.

Earlier on in this section, I explained the difference between the North and South Nodes in transit, and how North Node transits point to developing something that may feel unfamiliar with or getting out of your comfort zone, while South Node transits are about releasing anything no longer serving you and moving past old patterns holding you back. However, when timing relationship activity, it doesn't matter so much which one is transiting which house. You will still see events happen with either. For instance, if you have the South Node transiting your seventh house instead of the North Node, you can still expect significant events to occur in your love life. So, to keep it simple for now, don't fixate so much on what specific Node is transiting where, but rather simply take note of where you're seeing the Nodes transit in your chart in general.

The Nodes also take approximately 18 years to transit through all 12 signs in your chart, but since there are two Nodes, every nine years they will return to the same pair of signs. Therefore, you can observe a particular area of your life in nine-year increments, noting how similar events may reappear each time. For example, if you underwent a major life change like moving to a new city and having a total career change in the year 2015, when the Nodes were transiting the tenth house (career) and the fourth house (home) of your chart, you can know that nine years later in the year 2024, you may be itching for a job change or wanting to move homes once again. Now, let's apply that same train of thought to timing relationships.

NODES TRANSITING THE HOUSES

Let's start by zooming in on the Nodes moving through the first and seventh houses of your chart. Since the North and South Nodes transit a set of signs and houses at the same time, if one is transiting your seventh house, the other will always be transiting your first house. We have learned that the seventh house is associated with committed partnerships and the first house is your identity and sense of self, so the Nodes transiting through these two houses will see changes happen to both of those areas simultaneously. Changes that happen in one may inform developments that then take place in the other.

Nodal transits through your first and seventh houses point to a period where you're balancing your own goals while also tending to relationship matters. Over the course of the 18 months the Nodes spend in these two houses of your chart, you might rediscover the traits that make you unique or lean into interests that have been lying dormant for years. You will also be gaining greater confidence in yourself and learning how to enjoy your own company. A common cliché is that relationships happen when you're least expecting them. That statement definitely rings true with the first and seventh house Nodal transits because you're usually so busy figuring out who you are or entering into a major new chapter in your life that you aren't fixating so much on when you might meet someone. With this transit, you are prioritizing yourself more, and therefore your perspective on dating and relationships changes. You may end up raising your standards, deciding that you will or won't put up with certain behaviors from a potential partner. These Nodal transits open your eyes up to undertaking relationships differently. Since the ascendant and descendant lines fall within your first and seventh houses, you will want to take note of when the Nodes reach the exact degree of these angles in your chart. When that happens, the themes I'm mentioning here for these Nodal transits will intensify.

Though having the Nodes transiting through the first and seventh houses is very common when people meet their life partner, get married, or have their first child together, it isn't a given that these types of events will happen. Even if you don't have your happily ever after during this period, you will still end up learning something significant about yourself as well as realizing how you need to go about relationships differently moving forward. The last time I had the Nodes transiting my first and seventh houses was during the years 2017–19 when they were in Leo and Aquarius. I didn't meet the love of my life at this time, but two flings I had completely changed how I saw myself. Through one, I realized that I could paint, and I rediscovered creative skills that I hadn't utilized since I was 12 years old. The other was a short-lived fling who ghosted me, and my obsession with hearing back from him led me to discover astrology, which changed my entire life trajectory. The moral of the story is to stay open-minded as to what may come up within relationships during these Nodal transits. You can't entirely predict what will happen in that area of your life—all you can expect is that something will change there.

I want to linger on how the first and seventh house Nodal transits don't always result in a happy relationship event. It might be that the ending of a relationship forces you to become more independent, and you're automatically spending time alone rediscovering what lights you up because you aren't sharing that time with a partner. It may also be that, if a relationship has felt stagnant or you haven't had the courage to decide whether you want to stay with someone, these Nodal transits will definitely shake things up. As we will learn in Chapter 18 with example charts, the Nodes transiting the first and seventh house can really go either way, depending on your current life circumstances.

There are also a couple of other relevant Nodal transits for relationships. When the North and South Nodes transit the fifth and eleventh houses, there is usually greater romance going on, and your sex life tends to be more active. In addition, you are building your self-esteem when dating and figuring out what you do and don't want. At the same time, you're widening your social network, so it may mean that you're introduced to someone by a friend, or by dating someone new you are meeting people you otherwise wouldn't.

In contrast, having the Nodes transit your second and eighth houses is often a challenging time for a relationship. It might be that your partner is going through a difficult period where they need more of your support, or there could be stress surrounding shared money and finances. There may also be issues within a relationship that make you more aware of your own patterns that you want to heal and transform. Going to therapy for the first time is not uncommon with this Nodal transit. Even though having the Nodes transiting through your second and eighth houses can be trickier than the other house transits I mentioned, I still do see it frequently when a couple gets married because they have to learn how to share more of their life together and take care of practical matters, like opening a joint bank account.

TRANSIT NODES MAKING AN ASPECT
TO YOUR INNER PLANETS

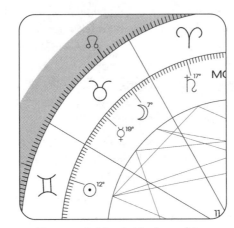

**The transit North Node making
a conjunction to the moon.**

No matter where your moon and Venus are located in your chart, having either of the Nodes transit over these two planets will likely bring up greater relationship activity for about a year or two. In the diagram above, you can see the transit North Node transiting over the moon in someone's chart. It's like the themes of these two planets get awakened and become more relevant for you during that time. Venus symbolizes relationships, friendships, and money, so you may experience change to any or all of those areas. This might mean getting into a relationship, taking the next step with your partner, or ending a relationship. Meanwhile, the moon is representative of your emotions and your home, so with one of the Nodes transiting over your moon, you may see a change to you and your partner's living situation or families. You may also be reflecting on how you express your feelings within a relationship, or you might be made aware of certain habits you've picked up in childhood and now carry into your adult relationships. Finally, you will also want to watch out for when the Nodes transit over your seventh house ruler.

For example, if you have a Pisces-ruled seventh house, then the Nodes transiting over Jupiter in your chart would be an important time for relationships as well.

Now that we've gone over the transits of Saturn, Jupiter, and the Nodes, you may want to take some time to look at past transits of your chart, pulling up dates for when a relationship was formed or went through a super happy period, as well as dates for when you experienced troubles in a relationship or went through a break-up. Write down or make a mental note of what parts of your chart Saturn, Jupiter, and the Nodes were moving through during those times.

Seeing what transits were happening during particularly difficult relationship periods can be quite therapeutic, as it may help you to realize that a break-up actually wasn't your fault and that there was nothing you could have done differently; that particular year may have always been meant to be challenging for your love life. On the other end of the spectrum, if you're looking at future transits, you may notice that you have a positive relationship year coming up soon, so you can stop putting so much pressure on yourself to be constantly dating or looking for someone. In addition, I want to mention that the more of these transits you have going on at the same time, the more significant that specific period becomes. For instance, having Jupiter transit your seventh house while Saturn or the Nodes are transiting over your moon or Venus at the same time is more likely to result in a major relationship event than just having Jupiter transit your seventh house on its own.

CHAPTER 17

Exact Timing

We just went over periods of one to three years that can be either positive or difficult for relationships. However, that is still quite a big time frame to take into consideration, and you might be curious to know what exact month or even week out of that period to zoom in on. So, I want to introduce a final technique for how to narrow down the exact timing of a relationship event. This is where transits get more advanced, because you're looking at several different moving parts. So, if you're confused at first by what I'm about to go over, do not worry. It takes time to get the hang of blending all of these pieces together.

When we looked at the transits of Saturn, Jupiter, and the Nodes, we saw that they spend a set amount of time transiting through a house of your chart or over a specific planet in your chart, like the moon or Venus. Let's take Saturn transiting through your seventh house as an example. Saturn will spend about three years in this house, but it's not like every day you'll wake up and feel like you're learning intense and challenging relationship lessons or seeking greater commitment with someone. Out of that entire three years, there will be a handful of weeks and months where those themes are intensified and become more prominent in your life. To narrow in on a more exact date of when you might meet someone, get engaged, or have an important realization about a relationship, you will want to track when there is a new or full moon or Mars meeting up with that Saturn transit. The shorter transits of the lunar phases and Mars awaken the full effects of transit Jupiter, Saturn, and the Nodes. Let's look at some visuals so you can better understand what I'm talking about.

A FRESH POTENTIAL: NEW MOONS

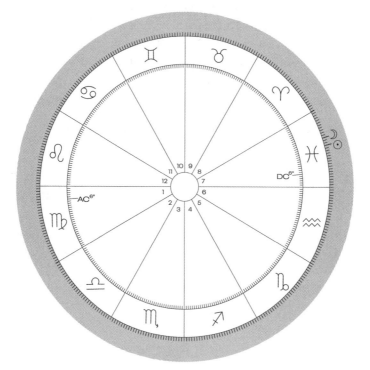

A new moon taking place in the seventh house.

Every month, there is one new moon and one full moon. A new moon happens when the sun and moon meet up with each other in transit in the same sign. It symbolizes a new beginning, and in the days that immediately follow a new moon, you may notice that different opportunities, relationships, or habits are formed. Additionally, a new moon can sometimes represent an ending, as you close one chapter in your life to start fresh for the next month. If you have a Virgo rising and a Pisces-ruled seventh house, you will experience a new moon in your seventh house during Pisces season, when the sun and moon meet up in that sign, as shown in the diagram above. When a new moon occurs in a relationship part of your chart like your fifth, seventh, or eighth house or in the same sign as your sun, moon, or Venus, you will be building upon the themes associated with that house or planet for a period of several weeks. You might start dating someone new and get clear on what you want out of a relationship, or you may be entering into an exciting new life chapter with your partner. You could also just want to prioritize the relationship more than you have been.

HEIGHTENED ACTIVITY: FULL MOONS

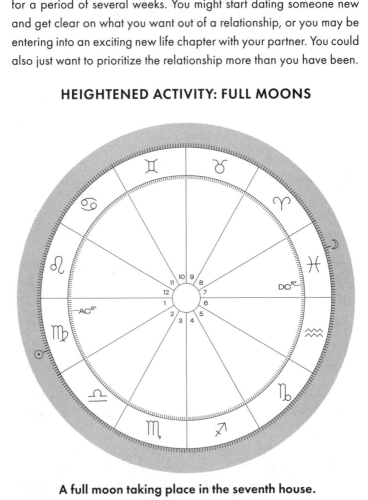

A full moon taking place in the seventh house.

A full moon occurs when the sun and moon oppose each other in transit, meaning they are in opposite signs, as shown in the diagram to the left. This lunar phase represents a culmination of activity, as well as seeing visible progress and results. At the time of the full moon each month, you may find yourself connecting with other people more than usual or realizing what area of your life you need to make adjustments to. The full moon can also bring up a lot of emotions, as you realize who or what isn't working for you anymore. If you know what zodiac "season" it currently is, you will know that the full moon that month will take place in the opposite sign. Going back to that same example of a Virgo rising chart, you will experience a full moon in Pisces, your seventh house, when it is Virgo season and the sun is in your first house. When a full moon occurs in a relationship part of your chart such as your fifth, seventh, or eighth house, or in the same sign as your sun, moon, or Venus, you may make important realizations about what you want out of a relationship, or you could reach a pivotal turning point where you're either getting closer to your partner or someone you've been seeing, or you're letting go of a relationship that is no longer working.

Though there will be one new moon and full moon in a specific house and sign of your chart every year, the new and full moons take on greater importance when a slower transit like Jupiter, Saturn, or the Nodes is moving through that part of your chart as well. The new or full moon will amplify the already existing transits of Jupiter, Saturn, and the Nodes for a particular month. So, out of the entire 12 months Jupiter spends in the seventh house, for instance, it is not until a new moon or full moon also takes place in the seventh house that you will likely experience a positive new relationship starting or something significant taking place within an existing relationship.

You can do the same exercise with a new or full moon happening in tandem with Saturn or the Nodes, too. Additionally, when a new moon or full moon falls close to the North or South Node, it would be an eclipse. A new moon paired with a Node is a solar eclipse, and a full moon paired with a Node is a lunar eclipse. Also, if you happen to have planets or an angle in the house that a new moon or full moon is falling in, take note of how far away the new or full moon is in degrees from that planet or angle. The closer a lunation happens to a birth chart placement, the more significant it will be for you. You will feel the effects of the new or full moon much more intensely than you would without a planet or angle there.

TAKING ACTION: MARS

Transit Mars indicates what you're putting energy toward during the six-week period it spends in a particular house of your chart. You may have more motivation to tackle problems, confront issues head on, and get things done in that part of your life. You're seeing more action take place with the themes represented by whatever house or planet Mars is transiting. However, Mars transits are not the lightest energy. When Mars enters a new house of your chart or connects with a planet in your birth chart, there might be tension to address, or inner frustrations could come up. You will want to take action, though. If you've been hesitant to make a decision regarding a relationship or take the next step with your partner, Mars will urge you to do just that.

Similar to how we can track the new and full moons with the transits of Jupiter, Saturn, and the Nodes, you can do the same with Mars. When Mars meets up with those longer transits, it will call greater attention to them. It may also aggravate these transits, so you may feel an intense pressure to do something differently in a relationship or address any underlying problems you've been ignoring with your partner. Because of Mars' aggressive tendencies, it's common to see a Mars transit going on in a relationship part of your chart at the time of a break-up or when there's more fighting going on with your partner.

Not only is it important to note when Mars meets up with Jupiter, Saturn, or a Node in a relationship house or on a planet like your sun, moon, or Venus, but you will also want to pay attention to when Mars forms a square or opposition to those same transits. For example, if Saturn is transiting your seventh house, then the Mars transit of your first, fourth, and tenth houses, where it is making a 90-degree square to that Saturn transit, will also put the significations of that Saturn seventh house transit into motion. Hard aspects like the square or opposition cause just as much to happen as a conjunction. If you need a refresher on how to identify aspects, you can turn to page 87. You will also have a better idea of what I'm talking about when we get to some chart examples in the next chapter.

CHAPTER 18

Relationships in Real Life: Chart Examples

We just went over a lot of information, so let's take what we've learned about transits thus far and put it into practice! The best way to learn about astrology is by seeing it play out in real peoples' lives. Through the following client examples and chart diagrams, you will be able to see how these transits work together. First, we will go over which of the transits were happening when people got into a relationship, got engaged, or married. Next, we will see how some of those same transits resulted in a break-up or divorce for other people.

FINDING LOVE AFTER BEING CHRONICALLY SINGLE

I'm using my own chart as an example first, because I used to think that I would be single forever and didn't actually believe anything would happen when my relationship houses were activated with transits. My mindset was that no relationship had ever lasted for me before, so why would that suddenly change? I was not on any dating apps because by that point I hated them, and since starting my astrology business I barely had time to socialize or do anything outside of work, so it was not like I was making an effort to meet people in real life. I learned how to read a transit chart in 2018, though, so I had known in advance that 2021 would be a good year for me romantically due to Jupiter and Saturn transiting my seventh house, and the North Node moving through my fifth at the same time. Then Covid happened, which diminished all hope of me meeting someone anytime soon. I knew these positive relationship transits were coming up for me, though, in 2021, so I was almost willing the universe to make something happen. If I was meant to meet someone, it would have to appear out of nowhere, because I was putting in zero effort.

When Jupiter and Saturn moved into my seventh house in December 2020, I made a vow to myself that I was done with all of my previous dating habits. I was tired of pining after guys who were clearly not interested, and I no longer wanted to casually sleep with people I barely knew. I made a list of all the traits I wanted in a long-term partner, focusing on how I wanted to feel around them, rather than surface-level traits like the color of their hair or their job title. Saturn moving into my seventh house helped me get serious about what I was looking for in a relationship, and I was able to see how I needed to clear outdated patterns and mindsets from this area of my life. Jupiter transiting my seventh house also urged me to keep an open mind to meeting people who weren't my usual type. As I mentioned in the introduction to this book, in late January 2021, a week after my 28th birthday, when New York was still partially locked down because of a Covid resurgence, I had a random message from an Instagram follower, saying that she had a male friend she thought I would get along with and asking if I wanted to be connected with him. I said yes, and our first date took place on February 11, 2021. The top chart on the following page shows the transits that were happening to my birth chart on that particular date.

Our first date took place on the night of a new moon in Aquarius, which you can see along with Jupiter, Saturn, and several other planets transiting my seventh house. Even though Jupiter and Saturn had been in my seventh house since the end of December, it took until that new moon almost two months later for those transits to be fully activated for me. If we want to get into even greater specifics for that particular date, Jupiter was almost exactly conjunct with my descendant line.

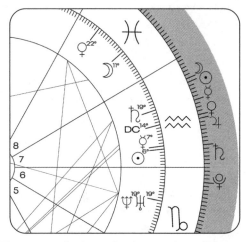

**New moon in Aquarius in my seventh house.
Jupiter and Saturn also transiting the seventh house.**

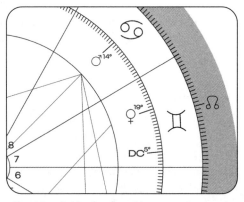

**The North Node transiting my partner's
seventh house and his Venus.**

I've mentioned before how the angles act as sensitive points within the houses they are located. So having Jupiter reach the exact degree of my descendant was also going to be the most important time period out of its entire 12-month transit of my seventh house. As a final note, the North and South Nodes were transiting my fifth and eleventh houses, bringing in another relationship transit. So, you can see how in order for something very significant in my love life to take place, like meeting the man who would later become my boyfriend, several of the transits we just discussed were simultaneously taking place.

Now, if we were to look at my partner's chart below mine on the opposite page for that exact same date, he had the North Node transiting over his Venus in Gemini in his seventh house, while the South Node was transiting his first. With the Nodal transit through his seventh house paired with a Nodal transit to his Venus, that time period was also bound to be significant for him romantically. It's a fun exercise to see how events can show up in your partner's transit chart, too, because the transits will be similar but different.

A RELATIONSHIP HAPPENING
WHEN YOU LEAST EXPECT IT

A similar situation happened with one of my clients, Madison. She had come to me for an astrology reading in April 2021, after having just gone through a break-up. She was not interested in jumping back into a relationship anytime soon, so she didn't really believe me when I said I saw a lot of romantic activity coming up later that year, specifically in August. Like me, Madison has a Leo rising, so she also had Jupiter and Saturn transiting her seventh house throughout 2021, and the North Node transiting her fifth house as well. On top of that, she had Venus in Aquarius in her seventh house in her birth chart, which would also get activated by the transits of Jupiter and Saturn. The reason I highlighted August as a date to look out for was that there were a rare two full moons in Aquarius taking place from the end of July to the end of August in her seventh house, awakening those longer Jupiter and Saturn transits for her. I would have been shocked if something hadn't happened!

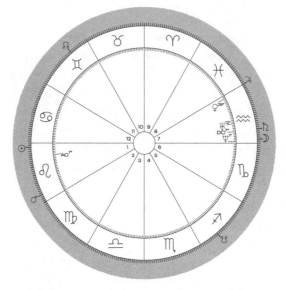

**First full moon in Aquarius in the seventh house.
Transit Saturn conjunct the descendant line.**

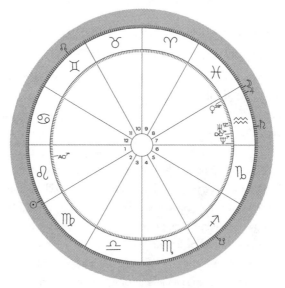

**Second full moon in Aquarius in the seventh
house aligned with transit Jupiter.**

In July, Madison reconnected with someone she had known since middle school on a dating app, and their first date took place on July 18. From the start, she knew she wanted something serious with this person (fitting with the Saturn seventh house transit), but she still wasn't sure if she was ready for another relationship. She didn't want to be so quick to sacrifice her independence, so she broke things off. The universe had other plans, though. On July 23, the first of two full moons in Aquarius took place in her seventh house and was exactly aligned with the ongoing Saturn transit there. See the diagram to the left. During that full moon, she realized that she wanted to give it another go, and on July 29, they rekindled their romance. By the second full moon in Aquarius on August 21, she was posting about their relationship on Instagram, and the relationship has been strong ever since.

Looking at the two transit charts to the left for Madison, I want to point out a few different elements. In the top diagram for the first full moon in Aquarius that took place in her seventh house, notice how close Saturn is to her descendant line. Out of the entire three years that Saturn transited Madison's seventh house, Saturn was felt the most intensely around this date, because of its proximity to her descendant. In the bottom diagram, for the August 21 full moon in Aquarius, I want you to shift your attention to transiting Jupiter, which has moved backward because it's retrograde, and it is right on top of Madison's Venus in Aquarius. The full moon occurred in exact alignment with transiting Jupiter on that day, triggering the Jupiter–Venus transit which was already taking place. Both of these charts perfectly illustrate how full moons can awaken the potential of transiting Jupiter and Saturn. Because a full moon also symbolizes a culmination of activity, where you're usually seeing visible results and making important realizations, it is not surprising that Madison had a lot of feelings about the relationship at this time and was making the decision of whether or not to continue dating her now partner.

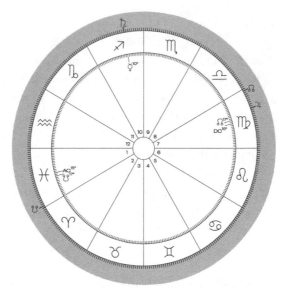

**Jupiter and the North Node transiting
Zoe's seventh house in Virgo.**

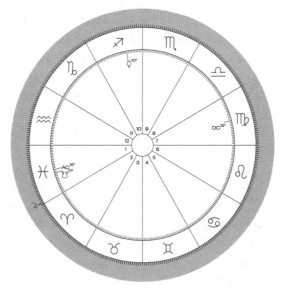

Jupiter transiting Zoe's first house in Pisces.

FROM HIGH SCHOOL SWEETHEARTS
TO HUSBAND AND WIFE

For relationships that have been going on for a longer period of time, you will start to see the same transits come back around again. Patterns will repeat themselves within the relationship, and you will notice how the same transit will result in similar circumstances or events happening in the relationship. Take Zoe for instance. She first got together with her now husband in November of 2015, when they were both seniors in high school. In the top chart on the opposite page, you can see that Jupiter and the North Node were transiting her seventh house. Saturn was simultaneously transiting through Sagittarius, where the ruler of Zoe's seventh house, Mercury, is located. That makes three important transits happening at once: the North Node in the seventh, Jupiter in the seventh, and Saturn aspecting the ruler of the seventh.

Fast-forward to November 2022, when Zoe got married to her high school sweetheart. Once again, Jupiter was transiting a prominent part of her chart, seen in the bottom chart on the opposite page. Jupiter had made its way from transiting her seventh house in 2015 to transiting her first house in 2022, and it resulted in Zoe reaching another happy relationship milestone. Because the first and seventh houses are opposite to one another, transits through either are felt similarly. As Jupiter makes its way back to Zoe's seventh house from 2027–28, I would expect a positive turning point in the relationship to happen yet again.

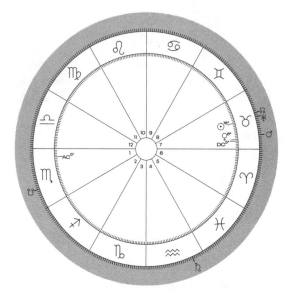

**The North Node, Mars, and Uranus transiting
the seventh house in Taurus.**

CALLING OFF AN ENGAGEMENT

In a couple of the previous examples, the Nodes transiting the first and seventh houses resulted in the person getting into a new relationship. However, these same Nodal transits are often not that easy, which we will look at in Sophia's chart. The Nodes transiting through relationship-oriented parts of the chart result in change, which can sometimes be good, but in other cases can result in unexpected, difficult changes. Again, you will want to examine how you're feeling about a current relationship when Nodal transits like the ones I discuss here begin. Astrological transits are simply reflecting back what you already know deep down but may not want to readily admit yet.

Sophia is a Scorpio rising, with a Taurus sun and Venus in her seventh house. In the spring of 2021, she got engaged to her long-term boyfriend, whom she had been dating since 2015. A year later, though, in July 2022, her partner suddenly called off the engagement. Sophia said that the break-up came as a complete surprise, but the more I asked about the transits that had been going on in her chart in the year leading up to July 2022, she admitted that they had been having problems for a while. In the weeks leading up to the break-up, she had felt like her partner didn't appreciate the type of career she had, and there was also conflict and uncertainty coming up around their finances and living situation. Let's look at the transits in Sophia's chart to the left to see why all of these issues finally came to a head in July.

In the transit chart on the opposite page, you can see the North Node transiting through Sophia's seventh house and moving across her sun in Taurus at the exact same degree. So just from that transit, you would know that this time period would be very relationship-focused for her. However, Mars is also in Taurus, meeting up with the North Node and Uranus there. As we've learned, transit Mars tends to create conflict and irritability and urges you to confront any issues you've been sweeping under the rug. Mars entered Taurus, Sophia's seventh house, on July 5 and remained there until August 20, which was indicative of tensions escalating in the relationship during that time frame. All of the problems Sophia and her then fiancé had been able to work through before came back up again, but this time they could not be resolved. I also mentioned how Mars can symbolize separation or making a quick decision, which describes the sudden nature of Sophia's break-up, too.

One last aspect I wanted to note is that Saturn is transiting through Aquarius, square to Sophia's sun and Venus in Taurus. That transit had been going on throughout all of 2021 and 2022 and was indicative of having increased stress in the relationship. Saturn squaring her sun and Venus tested the relationship, making the ways in which it wasn't working much more obvious.

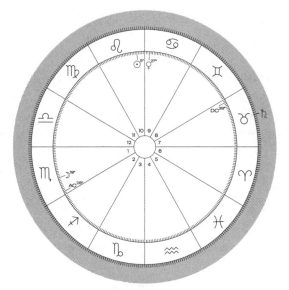

Saturn transiting the seventh house in 1999.

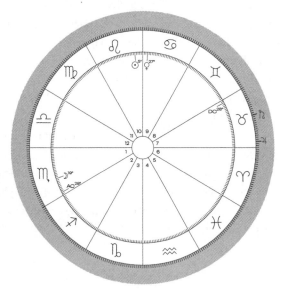

Jupiter and Saturn transiting the seventh house in 2000.

LETTING GO OF ONE RELATIONSHIP
TO WELCOME ANOTHER

Similar to Sophia, the transiting Nodes played a key role in the ending of a relationship for Kristen, when she got divorced. Kristen is a Scorpio rising, with a Scorpio moon in the first house. Therefore, transits through the first and seventh houses of her chart will affect her moon as well. Kristen married her first husband in autumn 1992. By 1999, her marriage was on the rocks when she realized she didn't want to move to a different state with him, and she started questioning their future. In the top diagram to the left, you can see that in 1999 Saturn was moving through her seventh house, bringing up greater relationship tension, as she faced the reality of the underlying problems she was having with her husband. Themes involving her home were coming up, too, because Saturn's transit through her Taurus seventh house was opposing her Scorpio moon at the same time. She ultimately decided to stick it out with her husband, and they ended up moving to another city together in the year 2000. By that year, Jupiter had also entered Taurus, Kristen's seventh house, alleviating some of the pressure that was caused by Saturn. This can be seen in the lower diagram to the left. She entered into a brief happy time in the relationship again, when she thought things might be looking up.

However, the same problems began to resurface. At the end of 2000 and into 2001, Jupiter moved into Gemini, Kristen's eighth house. Also, in 2001 and 2002, the North Node was transiting Gemini. With two eighth house activations going on one after the other, Kristen entered into another challenging period in her relationship. Reflecting on that period, she says that it became very clear that the relationship was going nowhere, and she could no longer convince herself otherwise. Eighth house transits often amplify relationship problems. It took until March 2003, at the end of the North Node's transit through her eighth, for Kristen to work up the courage to ask for a divorce. A few months earlier, in November 2002, a lunar eclipse had taken place at 28 degrees of Taurus (as

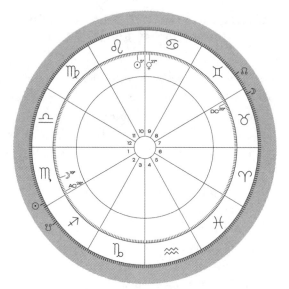

**A lunar eclipse in Taurus on the descendant line.
November 2002.**

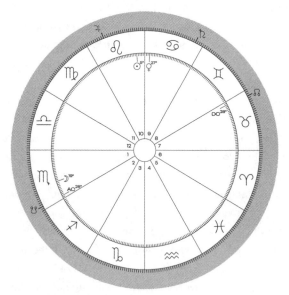

The North Node transiting the descendant line in July 2003.

shown in the top diagram on the opposite page), the same degree as Kristen's descendant line in her seventh house. A lunar eclipse is like a supercharged full moon, where it brings up important realizations and visible activity, but unlike a full moon, the themes associated with a lunar eclipse tend to play out over a several-month period, and the changes brought about tend to be more major. That lunar eclipse in her seventh pushed Kristen to finally realize she wanted to end her marriage.

Kristen's story ends on a happy note, though. In July 2003, a few months after her divorce was finalized, she ended up meeting the man who is now her husband. Looking at the diagram from that time on the bottom of the opposite page, the North Node had just moved fully into Taurus and was at 28 degrees, conjunct to her descendant line. The South Node was in Scorpio, conjunct to her Scorpio moon next to her ascendant. There were other significant transits taking place, too. Jupiter was transiting through Leo, Kristen's sun sign, and simultaneously squaring her Scorpio moon, signaling a happy year in her personal life, when she was feeling more optimistic and freer. Meanwhile, Saturn had entered Cancer and was creeping up on a conjunction to Kristen's Venus in Cancer, meaning another round of important relationship lessons were on the way. By tracking the transits to Kristen's chart over the course of this four-year period, from 1999 to 2003, we have seen the many twists and turns a person's love life can take, and how some of these transits build upon each other. Transiting Jupiter, Saturn, and the Nodes all played a role in the ending of one relationship and the beginning of another.

One final point I want to make about all of these chart examples is that, in each case, the planets were not causing any of these relationship events to happen out of nowhere. Astrological transits are not something you should fear. When these relevant transits came up for each person, they simply amplified the feelings that were already there in the relationship. In my own example, I was desiring a committed relationship and focusing on the traits I wanted in a partner when I happened to meet my now boyfriend. For the first time in my life, I finally felt ready to be in a serious relationship and my transits reflected that. In the case of Madison, she already knew she felt serious about her now partner, the full moon just gave her a nudge to act on those feelings. In the examples of both Sophia and Kristen, they were made more aware of underlying relationship issues that they had previously brushed off or hadn't fully dealt with. I cannot emphasize this enough: if you are already in touch with your intuition and what your gut instincts are telling you, none of these transits will come as a huge surprise.

Final Thoughts

If you've made it to the end of this book, you should be proud of yourself! We have gone over quite a bit of astrology, from learning the basics of reading your birth chart all the way to understanding the complexities of astrological transits. I hope this is a book you will be able to return to time and time again, learning new tidbits of information here and there. Studying astrology is a lifelong practice, so if some of the chapters in this book went over your head, it won't always be that way. The more time you spend observing how certain signs or planets manifest in people's personalities as well as in your own life, the more information you can add to your encyclopedia of astrology knowledge.

When writing this book, I thought about what type of astrology resource I wish I had had when I was first getting started. I remember initially researching some of my chart placements, like Saturn in the seventh house, and dwelling on all of the negative interpretations written about it online. I worried that a placement like this meant my love life was a lost cause and I was destined to be alone forever. Over time, I came to realize that that was certainly not the case, and I learned how to embrace my chart and how it was uniquely me, instead of fixating on all of the areas in which I faced difficulties. Within the relationship I have now with my current partner, as well as other close relationships in my life like with my parents or my friends, occasionally I will revisit my birth chart to help me understand why I am having certain reactions and how I can transform any outdated behaviors. Astrology has helped me to accept myself, which in turn has improved my relationships.

I hope that you, too, have realized that nothing in your chart means you are doomed in love. My biggest wish is that from reading this book, you have gained a greater awareness of your relationship patterns and a better idea of what you want for yourself in your love life. Remember, you have the power to choose who you want to date and what you want out of a relationship. No amount of sign compatibility with another person can determine if a relationship will or will not work—that is something you have to decide for yourself. Relationships are complex, and the astrology we have learned simply reflects that. Knowing a person's sun sign only scratches the surface of who that person really is, and even if you figure out all of the other signs, houses, planets, and aspects in someone's chart, there is still no one-size-fits-all interpretation for any of these placements. Instead of letting astrology dictate your romantic decisions, you now know that you can use it as a guide to better understand your partner and figure out if you are getting everything you need out of a relationship.

By now, you are not only able to walk away feeling more confident in your romantic decisions, but you have also realized that your relationship timing is specific to you. Instead of blaming yourself for failed relationships or not being in the same place romantically as some of your friends, you can be reassured that you are exactly where you are meant to be at this very moment. If there is one thing I want you to remember moving forward, it is to always trust your timing!

Acknowledgments

This book would not have been possible without the support of my online astrology community. Thank you to everyone who has had a reading with me, listened to my podcast, taken my workshops and courses, shared my social media posts, and purchased this book. I would not have an astrology business without you.

I will be forever indebted to my former literary agent, Emily Harris. She pushed so hard for this book to happen, and also helped me to come up with the title. Also, a huge thank-you to my editor, Ru Merritt, who understood my vision for this book from the start and let me explore astrology in a more complex way. It was clear from the moment we had our first meeting that you were the perfect person to edit it. Thank you as well to the whole team at Penguin Books who helped turn this book into a reality. And many thanks to my current agent, Rosie Pierce, for not being creeped out that I analyzed your entire birth chart before our first call, and for always being there to lend your perspective and advice.

In addition, I have to give a shout-out to all my closest friends and family who had to hear me complain about my dating drama for the longest time. You were always there to listen, and you never told me to just get over it, especially Christina, Maxine, Maddie, Nika, Lauren and my little sister, Julia. I'm especially grateful for my dad, Scott, and my stepmom, Karyn, who have both helped me to become a more spiritual and mindful person over the past few years.

And last, but certainly not least, thank you to the love of my life, Jesse, for accepting me just as I am, and for showing me what a healthy relationship looks like. I could not have dreamed of a more perfect partner.

About the Author

Photo © Julia Bell

Alice Bell is a full-time astrologer and resident astrologer for British *Vogue*. She first got into astrology because it helped her validate certain personality traits she had always had trouble accepting, but it also made her more aware of which areas of life she needed to lean into to feel more fulfilled. Through her work, she aims to help others find their unique life path and trust in their own personal timing.

In addition to her weekly horoscopes for British *Vogue*, she hosts the podcast *Astrology with Alice* and has worked with many fashion and beauty brands to create astrology content. Her work has been featured in *Vogue*, *Refinery29*, *goop*, the *New York Times*, and *Forbes*. She currently lives in Brooklyn, New York. You can find Alice on Instagram @stalkalice.

Trust Your Timing

First published by Ebury, a division of The Random House Group Ltd

Andrews McMeel Publishing
a division of Andrews McMeel Universal
1130 Walnut Street, Kansas City, Missouri 64106

www.andrewsmcmeel.com

23 24 25 26 27 KPR 10 9 8 7 6 5 4 3 2

ISBN: 978-1-5248-8817-6

Library of Congress Control Number: 2023943063

Editor: Katie Gould
Art Director: Diane Marsh
Production Editor: Meg Utz
Production Manager: Julie Skalla

ATTENTION: SCHOOLS AND BUSINESSES
Andrews McMeel books are available at quantity discounts with bulk purchase for educational, business, or sales promotional use. For information, please e-mail the Andrews McMeel Publishing Special Sales Department: sales@amuniversal.com.